I0542282

THE
BLACK CROSS

OLIVE M. BRIGGS

1st WORLD
LIBRARY
Literary Society

The Black Cross

Olive M. Briggs

© 1st World Library, 2007
PO Box 2211
Fairfield, IA 52556
www.1stworldlibrary.com
First Edition

LCCN: 2007930811

Softcover ISBN: 978-1-4218-4855-6
Hardcover ISBN: 978-1-4218-4758-0
eBook ISBN: 978-1-4218-4952-2

Purchase *"The Black Cross"*
as a traditional bound book at:
www.1stWorldLibrary.com/purchase.asp?ISBN=978-1-4218-4855-6

1st World Library is a literary, educational organization
dedicated to:

- Creating a free internet library of downloadable ebooks

- Hosting writing competitions and offering book publishing
scholarships.

Interested in more 1st World Library books? contact:
literacy@1stworldlibrary.com
Check us out at: www.1stworldlibrary.com

1st World Library Literary Society

Giving Back to the World

"If you want to work on the core problem, it's early school literacy."

- James Barksdale, former CEO of Netscape

"No skill is more crucial to the future of a child, or to a democratic and prosperous society, than literacy."

- Los Angeles Times

"Literacy... means far more than learning how to read and write... The aim is to transmit... knowledge and promote social participation."

- UNESCO

"Literacy is not a luxury, it is a right and a responsibility. If our world is to meet the challenges of the twenty-first century we must harness the energy and creativity of all our citizens."

- President Bill Clinton

"Parents should be encouraged to read to their children, and teachers should be equipped with all available techniques for teaching literacy, so the varying needs and capacities of individual kids can be taken into account."

- Hugh Mackay

TO

YAPHAH

PART I

CHAPTER I

It was night in St. Petersburg. The moon was high in the heavens, and the domes, crowned with a fresh diadem of snow, glittered with a dazzling whiteness. In the side streets the shadows were heavy, the facades of the great palaces casting strange and dark reflections upon the pavement; but the main thoroughfares were streaked as with silver, while along the quay all was bright and luminous as at noontide, the Neva asleep like a frozen Princess under a breast-plate of shimmering ice.

The wind was cold, the air frosty and gay with tinkling sleigh-bells. A constant stream of people in sledges and on foot filled the Morskaia, hurrying in the one direction. The great Square of the Mariinski was alive with a moving, jostling throng, surging backwards and forwards before the steps of the Theatre like waves on a rock; a gay, well-dressed, chattering multitude, eager to present their tickets, or buy them as the case might be, and enter the gaping doors into the brilliantly lighted foyer beyond.

It was ballet night, but for the first time in the memory of the Theatre no ballet was to be given. Instead of the "Premiere Danseuse," the idol of Russian society, a new star had appeared, suddenly, miraculously almost, dropped from a Polish Province, and had played himself into the innermost heart of St. Petersburg.

The four strings of his Stradivarius, so fragile, so delicate and slim, were as four chains to bind the people to him; four living wires over which the sound of his fame sped from city to city, from province to province, until there was no musician in all the Russias who could play as Velasco, no instrument like his with the gift of tears and of laughter as well, all the range of human emotions hidden within its slender, resinous body.

So the people said as they gossiped together on the steps: "The great Velasco! The wonderful Velasco!" And now he was on his way to Germany. It was his last concert, his "farewell."

The announcement had been blazoned about on red and yellow handbills for weeks. One Salle after the other had offered itself, each more commodious than the last; but they were as nothing to the demands of the box-office. The list grew longer, the clamourings louder; and at last the unprecedented happened. At the request of a titled committee under the signature of the Grand-Duke Stepan himself, the Mariinski, largest and most beautiful of theatres, had opened its doors to the young god; and the price of tickets went up in leaps like a barometer after a storm;—fifteen roubles for a seat, twenty—twenty-five—and finally no seat at all, not even standing-room.

The crowd melted away gradually; the doors of the foyer closed; the harsh cries of the speculators died in the distance. Behind the Theatre the ice on the canal glimmered and sparkled. The moon climbed higher and the bells of the Nikolski Church rang out clearly, resonantly above the tree-tops.

Scarcely had the last stroke sounded when a black sleigh, drawn by a pair of splendid bays, dashed out of a side street and crossed the Pozeluief bridge at a gallop. At the same moment a troika, with three horses abreast, turned sharply into the Glinki and the two collided with a crash, the occupants flung out on the snow, the frightened animals plunging and rearing in a tangled, inextricable heap.

The drivers rushed to the horses' heads.

"A pest on you, son of a goat!" screamed the one, "Have you eyes in the back of your head that you can't see a yard in front of you?"

"Viper!" retorted the other furiously, "Damnation on you and your bad driving! Call the police! Arrest the shark of an anarchist!"

Meanwhile the master of the black sleigh, a heavily built, elderly man, had picked himself out of a drift with the assistance of his lackey and was brushing the snow from his long fur cloak. A fur cap, pulled down over his eyes, hid his face, but his gestures were angry, and his voice was high and rasping.

"Where is the fellow?" he snarled, "Let me see him; let me see his face. Away, Pierre, I tell you, go to the horses! A mercy indeed if their legs are not broken. A pretty pass this, that one can't drive through the streets of the capital, not even incognito!—Call the police!"

The other gentleman, who seemed little more than a boy, stood by the overturned troika wringing his hands:

"Is it hurt, my little one, my treasure, is it scratched? Keep their hoofs away, Bobo, hold them still a moment while I raise one end."

He knelt in the snow and peered eagerly beneath the sleigh.

"Sacre—ment!" cried the older man, "What is he after? Quick, on him, Pierre! Don't let him escape."

The lackey moved cautiously forward, and then gave a sudden leap back as the boyish figure sprang to his feet, clasping a dark, oblong object in his arms.

"A bomb, a bomb! In the name of all the saints! If he should drop it they were doomed, they were dead men!"

The eyes of the lackey were bulging with terror and he stood riveted to the spot. In the meantime the young man had snatched out his watch and was holding it up into a patch of moonlight.

"Twenty past the hour!" he exclaimed, "and old Galitsin fuming, I'll be bound! I'll have to make a run for it. Hey, Bobo!"

As he spoke, an iron hand came down on his shoulder and he looked up amazed into a pair of eyes, small and black and crossed, flashing with fury.

"Drop it," hissed a voice, "and I'll throttle you as you stand! Traitor! Assassin! Your driver obeyed orders, did he? You knew? Vermin, you ran us down! How did you know? Who betrayed me?—Who?"

The youth stood motionless for a moment in astonishment. He was helpless as a girl in that vicious grasp that was bearing him under slowly, relentlessly. "For the love of heaven," he cried, "Let go my arm, you brute, you'll sprain a muscle! Be careful!"

"Drop it, and I swear by all that is holy—"

"You old fool, you curmudgeon, you coward of an old blatherskite!" cried the boy, "I wouldn't drop it for all the world, not if you went on your bended knees. Bobo, yell for the police! Don't you touch my wrist! Look out now! Of all unpleasant things—!

"Bobo, come here. Never mind the horses. I tell you he is ruining my arm!—Hey! Help! You're an anarchist yourself, you fool! Shout, Bobo, shout!"

In the struggle the two had passed from the shadow into the moonlight and they now confronted one another. The master of the black sleigh was still enveloped in his cloak, only the gleam of his eyes, small and black and crossed, was visible under the cap, his beaked nose and the upward twist of his grey mustache.

The youth stood erect and angry; his head was bare, thrown back as a young lion at bay, his dark hair falling like a mane, clustered in waves about his broad, overhanging brows; strange brows and strange eyes underneath. The mouth was sensitive, the chin short and rather full, the whole aspect as of some one distinguished and out of the ordinary.

They stared at one another for a moment and then the hand of the older man dropped to his side. "I beg your pardon," he said, with some show of apology in his tone, "Surely I must have made a mistake. Where have I seen you before? You are no anarchist; pray, pardon me."

The young man was feeling his arm ruefully: "Good gracious, sir," he said, "but you are hasty!—I never felt such a grip. The muscles are quite sore already, but luckily it is the left arm, otherwise, Bozhe moi[1], I vow I'd sue you!—If it were the fingers now, or the wrist—"

He took off his fur gloves and examined both hands carefully, one after the other. A scornful look came over the older man's face:

"There was no excuse, my friend, for the way your troika rounded that corner. Such driving is criminal in a public street. It's a mercy we weren't all killed! Still, you really must pardon me, these anarchist devils are everywhere nowadays and one has to take precautions. I was hurrying to the Mariinski."

Hardly were the words out of his mouth, when there came the snapping of two watch lids almost simultaneously, and both gentlemen gave a cry of consternation.

"Oh, the deuce!" exclaimed the boy, "so was I, and look at the time if you please; the House will be in an uproar!"

The older man hurried towards the already righted sleigh: "Most unfortunate," he fumed, "and to-night of all nights! The entire concert will be at a standstill. The rug, Pierre, quick the rug! Are the horses ready? Hurry, you great lumbering son of an ox!"

The boy had already leaped into the troika and was wrapping the fur robes about his knees. "We shall put in an appearance about the same time, sir," he called back carelessly over his shoulder. "You won't miss anything, not a note, if that will comfort you. Hey, Bobo, go ahead! The concert can't begin without me."

Olive M. Briggs

"Without you," interrupted the other, "eh, what—you? Tysyacha chertei[2]! What do you mean?"

The master of the black sleigh stood up suddenly and threw back his cloak with a haughty gesture. He was in uniform and his breast glittered with orders. His cap fell back from his face, and his eyes, small and black and crossed, his beaked nose, his grey upturned mustache, showed distinctly in the moonlight. The face was known to every Russian, young and old, rich and poor—the Grand-Duke Stepan.

The youth made a low obeisance; then he tossed the hair away from his brows and laughed: "True, your highness," he said with mock humility, "I should have said—'until we both get there,' of course. Your pardon, sire."

The Duke leaned forward: "Stop—!" he exclaimed, "Your face—certainly somewhere I have seen it—Wait!"

The driver of the troika reined in the panting horses three abreast. They pawed the snow, still prancing a little and trembling, their bits flecked with foam. The youth saluted with one hand carelessly, while with the other he grasped the dark, oblong object that was not a bomb.

"Au revoir, your Grace," he cried, "You have seen me before and you will see me again, to-night, if this arm of mine recovers—" He laughed:—"I am Velasco."

As he spoke the horses leaped forward and the troika, darting across the moonlight of the Square, disappeared into the shadows behind the Mariinski.

The Duke gazed after it petrified: "Velasco!" he said, "And I all but twisted his wrist!—Ye gods!

"Go on, Pierre, go on!"

The Theatre was superbly lighted, crowded from the pit to the gallery, from the orchestra chairs to the Bel-Etage with the cream of St. Petersburg aristocracy.

It was like a vast garden of colour.

The brilliant uniforms of the officers mingled with the more delicate hues of ecru and rose, sky-blue and palest heliotrope of the loggias. Fans waved here and there over the house, fluttering, flashing like myriads of butterfly wings. The stage was filled with the black and white of the orchestra and the musicians sat waiting, the conductor gnawing his long mustache in an agony of doubt and bewilderment.

Gradually a hush stole over the House. The fans waved less regularly; the uniforms and the more delicate hues whispered together, glancing first at a box on the first tier, which was still empty, and then at the stage door and back again.

Where was the Grand-Duke Stepan, and where was the star, the idol, the young god, who was to charm their hearts with his four strings?—for whom they had paid fifteen roubles, twenty—twenty-five until there wasn't a seat left, not even standing room; only the crimson-curtained Imperial Loggia in the centre, solitary, significant.

The time passed; the minutes dragged slowly.

Suddenly the curtains moved. An usher appeared and placed a chair. Another moment of silence; then a tall, grey-haired, military figure stepped to the front of the loggia and bowed to right and to left; his eyes, small and black and crossed, glancing haughtily over the throng. "At last!"—The applause was mechanical, in strict accordance with etiquette, but there was a relieved note in it and the thousands of straining eyes leaped back to the stage, eager and watchful.

All at once a small door in the wings opened slightly and a slim boyish figure strode across the boards, a mane of dark hair falling over his brows.

"Velasco!" A roar went up from the House—"Velasco! Ah—h—viva—Velas—co!"

Instantly, with a tap of his baton, the conductor motioned for silence, and then, with the first downward beat, the orchestra began the introduction to the concerto.

The young Violinist stood languidly, his Stradivarius tucked under his arm, the bow held in a slim and graceful hand. His dark eyes roamed over the brilliant spectacle before him, from tier to tier, from top to bottom. He had seen it all before many times; but never so beautiful, so vast an audience, such a glory of colour, such closeness of attention. Raising his violin, with a strange, dreamy swaying of his young body, Velasco drew the bow over the quivering strings in the first solo passage of the Vieuxtemps.

The tones rose and fell above the volume of the orchestra. The depth of them, the sweetness seemed to penetrate to the uttermost corner. A curious tenseness came over the listening audience. Not a soul stirred. The Grand-Duke sat motionless with his head in his hands. The strings vibrated to each individual heart-beat; the bow sighed over them, and with the last note a murmur and then a roar went up.

Velasco stirred slightly, dropped his bow and bowed, without raising his eyes. Then, hardly waiting for the app-lause to subside, the second movement began, slow and passionate. The notes became fuller and more sensuous. The hush deepened. The silence grew more intense; a strain of listening, a fixed eagerness of watching.

Suddenly, in the midst, the Violinist raised his head from his instrument, drawing the bow with a slow, downward, caressing pressure over the E string. His eyes, half veiled and dreamy, looked straight across the House into a loggia next to the Imperial Box, impelled thereto by some force outside of his own consciousness.

A girl with an exquisite flower-like face was leaning over the crimson rail, her gaze on his, fixed and intent. The gold of her hair glistened in the light. Her lips were parted, the bosom of her dress rising and falling; her small hands clasped.

Velasco gazed steadily for a moment; then he dropped his head again, and swaying slightly played on.

The bow seemed fairly to rend the strings. He toyed with the difficulties; his scales, his arpeggios were as a flash, a ripple of notes tumbling over one another, each one a pearl. His lion's mane caressed the violin; his cheek pressed it like a living thing, closely, passionately, and it answered like a creature possessed.

As the strings vibrated to the last dying note, the beauty of it, the virtuosity, the abandon, drove the House mad with enthusiasm. They rose to him; they shouted his name eagerly, impetuously.

"Velasco! Viva!—Velasco! Bravo—bravissimo!"

Over the packed Theatre the handkerchiefs waved like a myriad of white banners. The bravos redoubled. The women tore the flowers from their girdles to fling on the stage; they lay piled on the white boards about him, broken and sweet, their perfume filling the air.

The young Violinist bowed, his hand on his heart, smiled and bowed again. He went out by the little door, and then came back and bowed and bowed.

The House rose as one man.

"Velasco! Velas—co!" It was deafening.

Suddenly out of the uproar, out of the crowd and the din, from someone, from somewhere, a bunch of violets fell at his feet. He raised them to his lips with a smile. "Viva— Velas—co—o!" The clapping redoubled.

About the stems of the violets, twined and intertwined again, was a twist of paper. His eyes fell for an instant on the blotted words and then the stage door closed behind him. They were few and almost illegible.

"*Will you help me—life or death—tonight? Kaya.*" The rest was a blot. He scanned them again more closely and shook the hair from his eyes.

"Velasco! Velasco—Viva!"

When the young Violinist came forward for the third time, his dark eyes flashed to the eyes of the girl like steel to a magnet. They seemed to plead, to wrestle with him.

"*Will you help me—life or death—tonight? Kaya.*"

Did her lips move; was it a signal? Her hands seemed to beckon him. He bowed low to the loggia, like one in a trance, once, twice, their eyes still together. And then, suddenly, he wrenched himself away remembering the House, the shouting, cheering, waving House.

"Ah—h Velasco—o!"

Lifting his violin he began to play again slowly, dreamily, hardly knowing how or why, a weird, chanting Polish improvisation like a love song, a song without words. His eyes opened and closed again. Always that gaze, pleading, wrestling, that flower-like face, those clasped hands beckoning.

Who was she—Kaya? His heart beat and throbbed; he was suffocating. With a last wild and passionate note Velasco tore the bow from the strings; it was as though the earth had opened and swallowed him up; he was gone.

[1] My God.

[2] A thousand devils!

CHAPTER II

In one of the poorer quarters of St. Petersburg there is a street on a back canal, and over the street an arch. To the right of the arch is a flight of steps, ancient and worm-eaten, difficult of climbing by day by reason of a hole here, a worn place there, and the perilous tilting of the boards; at night well nigh impassable without a lantern. The steps wind and end in a tenement, once a palace, spanning the water.

It was midnight.

A cloud had come over the moon, light and fleecy at first, but gradually growing blacker and spreading until finally it hung like a huge drop-curtain screening the stars.

The street lay in darkness. From a window in the top of the arch a single light was visible, pale and flickering as the ray from a candle; otherwise the grey bulk of the building seemed lost in the shadows, lifeless and silent.

Suddenly the light went out.

"Hist—st!" As if at a signal something moved on the staircase, creeping forward, and then from the shadow of the tenement, from under the archway, emerged other shadows, moving slowly like wraiths, hesitating, stopping, losing themselves in the general blackness, and then stirring again; shadows within shadows creeping.

Presently a door at the top of the steps opened and shut. Every time it opened, a shadow passed through and another crept forward. No word was spoken, no sound; not a step creaked, not a board stirred. It was a procession of ghosts.

Behind the door was a long stone passage, narrow and dark like a cave. The shadows felt the walls with their hands softly, gropingly, but the hands were silent like the feet. Except for a hurried breathing in the darkness the passage seemed empty.

Beyond were more steps leading down, and another passage, and then a second door locked and barred. Before this door the shadows halted, huddled together. "Hist—st!" Instantly the floor under them began to quiver and drop, inch by inch, foot by foot, down a well of continued blackness. The minutes passed. They still dropped lower and lower, so low that they were now below the level of the canal; down, down into the very foundations of the tenement, once a palace. All of a sudden the darkness ceased.

The room into which the elevator entered was large, low-raftered and lighted by a group of candles at the far end. In the centre was a black table, and about the table thirteen chairs also black. The one at the head was occupied by a figure garbed in a cloak and hood, with a black mask drawn down to the lips. The other chairs were empty.

By the light of the candles the shadows now took shape, the one from the other, and twelve black-cloaked and hooded figures stole forward, also masked to the lips. They passed one by one before the seated mask, touching his hand lightly, fleetingly, as one dipping the fingers into holy water, and then around the table to their seats, each in turn, until all were placed.

Some of the figures were tall, broad-shouldered and heavy, others small and slight. From the height, the strength or delicacy of the chin, the shape and size of the hand, was it alone possible to distinguish the sex; the rest was shrouded in a mystery absolute and unfathomable.

As the last and thirteenth chair was filled, the mask at the head leaned forward and pointed silently to a dark object at the far end of the room about which the candles flickered and sparkled. It was a huge Black Cross suspended as above an altar. Below it lay an open bier, roughly hewn out of the stone, and across it a name in scarlet lettering. The bier was empty.

The twelve other masks turned towards the Cross, reading the name, and they made a sign with the hands in unison, a rapid crisscross motion over the breast, the forehead, the eyes, ending in the low murmur of a word, unintelligible, like a pledge. Then the first mask to the left rose and bowed to the Head.

"Speak," he said, "the truth, the whole truth and nothing but the truth. Of what is this man accused?"

There was a moment of silence, intense and charged with significance; then the mask spoke.

"In the province of Pskof there is a Commune. One night, last winter, the peasants rose without warning. They shot, they maimed, they hacked, they burned alive every Jew in the village, men, women and children; not one escaped. The police were behind them. The instigator of the police was—"

The Head raised his hand: "Do you know this for a fact, from personal information?"

"I know it for a fact, from personal information."

The first mask took his seat and the second rose, a gaunt figure, the shoulders bowed and crippled under the cloak. His voice was deep and full, with tones plaintive and penetrating.

"A month ago there were seven men arrested. They were taken to 'Peter and Paul' and thrust into dungeons unspeakable. They received no trial; they were convicted of no crime; they never saw their families again. Three of these men are now in the mines. Two are still in the cells. Two are dead."

"Why were they arrested and by whose order?"

"They were workmen who had attended a meeting of the Social Democrats and had helped to circulate Liberal papers. It was done by the order of—"

The third mask sprang to his feet. His fists were clenched, and he was breathing hard like one who has been running.

"It is my turn," he cried, "Let me—speak! You know—you haven't forgotten!—On the Tsar's birthday, a band of students marched to the steps of the Winter Palace. They went peacefully, with trust in their hearts, no weapon in their hands. They were surrounded by Cossacks, who beat them with knouts, riding them down. They were boys, some of them hardly out of the Gymnasium, the flower of our youth, brave sons of Russia ready to fight for her and die." He hesitated and his voice broke. "At the foot of the Alexander Column, they were mown down like grass without warning,

Olive M. Briggs

or mercy; their blood still sprinkles the stones. Many were killed, hundreds arrested, few escaped. At the head of the Cossacks rode—"

A sigh stirred the room deepening into a groan, and then came a hush. Some buried their faces in their hands, weeping silently behind the masks. After a while the Head raised his hand and the fourth rose, slowly, reluctantly, speaking in a woman's voice so faint and low it could scarcely make itself heard. The masks bent forward listening.

"Last week," it murmured, "the Countess Petrushka was suspected. She was torn from her home, imprisoned"—The voice grew lower and lower. "She was beaten—tortured by the guards; she never returned,—yesterday she was—buried." The voice broke into sobs. "The man who signed the paper was—"

So the trial went on amid the stillness, more and more solemn, more and more impressive, as one accusation followed the other in swift succession; the candles dropping low in their sockets, the light growing dimmer, the room larger and lower and more ghostly, the night waning.

In every case the name was left a blank; but in that strange pause, as if for judgment, the eyes of the masks sought the bier, resting with slow fascination on the words across it, gleaming scarlet beneath the flickering candles, vivid and red like blood.

The final accusation had been made. The twelfth and last mask had sunk back in his chair and the leader rose. The silence was like a pall over the table. When his voice broke through, it was sharp and stern, as the voice of a judge admonishing a court.

"You have all heard," he said, "You are aware of what this man has done, is now doing, will continue to do. Does he merit to live?—Has he deserved to die? For the sake of our country, our people, ourselves, deliberate and determine.— His fate rests in the hands of the *Black Cross*."

He bowed his head on his breast and waited. No one moved or spoke. At the far end of the room, the candles dripped one by one on the bier, falling lower and lower. Occasionally the wax flared up, lighting the darkness; then all was dim.

Suddenly, as from some mysterious impulse, the thirteen sprang to their feet, and again their hands flashed out in that curious crisscross motion over the breast, the forehead, the eyes, and a murmur went from mouth to mouth like a hiss.

"*Cmeptb*—Death!" rising into a sound so intense, so terri- fying, so muffled and suppressed and menacing, it was as the cry of an animal wounded, dying, about to spring. Falling on their knees, they remained motionless for a moment; then, following the leader, each stepped forward in turn and took their places about the bier.

The ceremony that followed was strange and solemn; one that no outside eye has ever gazed on, no lips have ever dared to breathe. They stood in the shadow of death, their own and another's. Their heads were bowed. Their bodies shook and trembled. With hands raised they took the oath, terrible, relentless, overpowering, gripping them from now on as in a vice; both sexes alike, with voices spent and faint with emotion.

"*In the name of the Black Cross I do now pledge myself, an instrument in the service of Justice and Retribution. On whomsoever the choice of Fate shall fall, I vow the sentence of Death shall be fulfilled, by mine own hands if needs be,*

Olive M. Briggs

without weakness, or hesitation, or mercy. And if by any untoward chance this hand should fail, I swear—I swear, before the third day shall have passed, to die instead—to die—instead."

The words ended in a whisper, low, intense, prescient of a woe not to be borne.

"I swear—I pledge myself—by mine own hands if needs be."

A sigh broke the stillness. The masks stirred, recovered themselves and bent over the bier, drawing out, one after the other, a slip of paper folded. There were thirteen slips. Twelve were blank; on one was a Black Cross graven.

They drew in silence; no start, no movement, no trembling of the muscles betrayed the one fated. Twelve drew blanks. Which of them had the Cross; which? They stared dumbly, questioningly, fearfully from one to the other. One was the assassin. Which? The answer was shrouded behind the masks.

Lower and lower the candles burned in their sockets, flickering fitfully. The room grew darker and the figures, cloaked and hooded, seemed to melt back into the shadows from whence they had emerged, less and less distinct, until finally the shadow was one, more and more vapoury, filling the darkness.

Suddenly, a scream cut the silence, like a knife rough and jagged. In a twinkling the lights went out. There was a scuffling, a struggling in the corridor, cries and shouting, the sound of wood splintering, the blows of an axe,—a rushing forward of heavy bodies and the trampling of feet. The doors burst open, and a cordon of police dashed over the wreckage, cursing, shouting—and then stopped on the threshold, staring in amazement and panting with mouths wide open.

"Oi!—Oi! Tysyacha chertei!"

The room was empty, dark, deserted save for an old woman, half-witted, who was crouching on the floor before the sacred Icon, rocking herself and mumbling. They questioned her, but she was deaf and answered at random:

"Eh, gracious sirs—my lords—eh? So old—so poor, so wretched! See, there is nothing!—A copeck, for the love of heaven—half a copeck—a quarter, only a little quarter! Ah! Rioumka vodki[1]—rioumka—vodki!"

The police brushed her aside and searched the room. In the corner was a low cot, hanging on a nail was an old cloak; on the table the remains of a black loaf and an empty cup. They searched and searched in vain; tapping the walls, tearing at the stone foundations, peering up at the rafters, tumbling over one another in their eagerness.

"Chort vozmi[2]—!" shouted the captain, "We are on the wrong track. The scream came from the other side. Head them off! Run, men, run! Here, this passage, and then straight ahead! Devil take the old beggar! Shut up, you hag, or I'll strangle you!—Head them off!"

Gradually the hurrying footsteps died away in the distance. The shouting ceased on the stairs. It was still as the grave, silent, deserted. The old woman glanced over her shoulder. She was still crouching before the Icon, rocking herself backwards and forwards; the beads of the rosary slipping through her fingers one by one; mumbling to herself.

Suddenly she stopped and listened. The rosary fell to the floor. Her eyes watched the wreckage of the doorway

Olive M. Briggs

closely, suspiciously, like an animal before a trap. The shadows encircled her, they were here, there, everywhere; but none moved, none crept.

Snatching a slip of paper from her bosom, she bent over it, her eyes dilated, her mouth twisted with agony. In the centre of the paper, clearly graven against the white, was a Black Cross.

She moaned aloud, wringing her hands. Her teeth gnawed her lips. She clung to the foot of the Icon, sobbing, struggling with herself, glancing around fearfully into the shadows. A gleam from the candle fell on her hood; it had slipped slightly and a strand of her hair hung from under the cowl. It sparkled like gold.

She staggered to her feet, still sobbing and trembling, catching her breath. Then she went to the nail on the wall and took down the cloak. The woman stood alone in the midst of the shadows; they were heavy, motionless. Glancing to right and left, behind her, to the wreckage of the door, to the furthermost corner, back to the Icon again, her eyes roved, darting from side to side like a creature hunted. Clasping the cloak to her quivering bosom she approached the candle slowly, stealthily. Her steps faltered. She hesitated. She stooped forward—another glance over her shoulder, and blowing with feeble breath, the spark went out.

[1] A small glass of brandy.

[2] "The devil take you!"

CHAPTER III

Velasco sat in his Studio before the great tiled fire-place, dreaming, with his violin across his knees. His servant had gone to bed and he was alone.

The coals burned brightly, and the lamp cast a golden, radiant light on the rug at his feet, rich-hued and jewel tinted as the stained rose windows of Notre Dame. Tapestries hung from the walls, a painting here and there, a few engravings. In the centre stood an Erard, a magnificent concert-grand, open, with music strewn on its polished lid in a confusion of sheets; some piled, some fluttering loose, still others flung to the floor where a chance breeze, or a careless hand, may have scattered them. Near it was the exquisite bronze figure of a young satyr playing the flute, the childish arms and limbs, round and molded, glowing rosy and warm in the lamp light. In one corner was a violin stand, a bow tossed heedlessly across it; and all about were boxes, half packed and disordered. The curtains were drawn. The malachite clock on the mantel-piece was striking two.

Velasco stirred suddenly and his dark head turned from the fire light, moving restlessly against the cushions. He was weary. The applause, the uproar of the Mariinski was still in his ears; before his eyes danced innumerable notes, tiny and black, the sound of them boring into his brain.

"Ye gods—ye gods!"

The young Violinist sprang up and began pacing the room, pressing his hands to his eyes to drive away the notes, humming to himself to get rid of the sound, the theme, the one haunting, irrepressible motive. He walked up and down, lighting one cigarette after the other, puffing once, twice, and then hurling it half-smoked into the coals.

Every little while he stopped and seemed to be listening. Then he went back to his seat before the fire-place and flinging himself down began to play, a few bars at a time, stopping and listening, then playing again. As he played, his eyes grew dreamy and heavy, the brows seemed to press upon them until they drooped under the lids, and his dark hair fell like a screen.

When he stopped, a strange, moody look came over his face and he frowned, tapping the rug nervously with his foot. Sometimes he held the violin between his knees, playing on it as on a cello; then he caught it to his breast again in a sudden fury of improvisation—an arpeggio, light and running, his fingers barely touching the strings—the snatch of a theme—a trill, low and passionate—the rush of a scale. He toyed with the Stradivarius mocking it, clasping it, listening.

His overwrought nerves were as pinpoints pricking his body. His brain was like a church, the organ of music filling it, thundering, reverberating, dying away; and then, as he lay back exhausted, low, subtle, insinuating ran the theme in his ears, the maddening motive.

Beside him was a stand, with a decanter of red wine and a glass. The wine was lustrous and sparkling. He drank of it, and lit another cigarette and threw it away. Presently Velasco took from his pocket a twist of paper blotted, and studied it, with his head in his hands.

"Will you help me—life or death—tonight? Kaya."

He listened again.

The theme was still running, the black notes dancing; but between them intertwined was a face, upturned, exquisite, the eyes pleading, the lips parted, hands clasped and beckoning. That night at the Mariinski—ah!

He had searched for her everywhere. Ushers had flown from loggia to loggia, ransacking the Theatre. Next to the Imperial Box, or was it the second? To the right?—no, the left! Below, or perhaps on the Bel-Etage?—All in vain. Was it only a dream? He stared down at the twist of paper blotted *"Kaya—to-night."*

Her name came to his lips and he repeated it aloud, smiling to himself, musing. His eyes gazed into the coals, dreamy, heavy, half open, gleaming like dark slits under the brows. They closed gradually and his head fell lower. His hands relaxed. The violin lay on his breast, his pale cheek resting against the arch.

He was asleep.

All of a sudden there came a light tap on the door. A pause, a tap, still lighter; then another pause.

Velasco raised his head and tossed back his hair restlessly; his eyes drooped again.

"Tap—tap."

He started and listened.

Some one was at the Studio door—something. It was like the flutter of a bird's wing against the oak, softly, persistently.

"Tap—tap."

He rose slowly, reluctantly to his feet and went to the door. It was strange, inexplicable. After two, and the moon was gone, the night was dark—unless—An eager look came into his eyes.

"Who is there?" he cried, "Who are you? What do you want?"

A silence followed, as if the bird had poised suddenly with wings outstretched, hovering. Then it came again against the oak: "Tap—tap."

Velasco threw open the door: "Bozhe moi!"

As he did so, a woman's figure, slim and small, hooded and wrapped in a long, black cloak, darted inside, and snatching the door from his hand, closed it behind her rapidly, fearfully, glancing back into the darkness. The woman was panting under the hood. She braced herself against the door, still clasping the bolt as though a weapon. Her back was crooked beneath the cloak and she seemed to be crippled.

Velasco drew back. His eagerness vanished and the light died out of his face. "Who in the name of—" He hesitated: "What in the world—" Then he hesitated again, his dark eyes blinking under his brows.

The woman stretched her hands from under the cloak, clasping them. She was fighting hard for her breath.

"Tell me, Monsieur," she whispered, "Tell me quickly—are you married? Are you going alone to Germany?" Her voice shook and trembled: "Oh, tell me,—quickly."

"Married, my good woman!" exclaimed Velasco. His eyes opened wide and he drew back a little further: "Why really, Madame—Of course I am going alone to Germany. What do you mean? How extraordinary!"

"Quite alone?" repeated the woman, "no friend, no manager? Oh then, sir, do me the little favour, the kindness—it will cost you nothing—I shall never forget it—I shall bless you all the days of my life."

She took a step forward, limping. Velasco recovered himself.

"Sit down, Madame," he said, "and explain. You are trembling so. Let me give you some wine.—Wait a minute. There,—is it money you want? Tell me."

His manner was that of a prince to a beggar, lofty, authoritative, kindly, indifferent. "Sit down, Madame."

The woman shrank back against the door and her hand fled to the bolt as if seeking support. "No—no!" she murmured. "You don't understand. It's not for—not money! I'm in trouble, danger. Don't you see? I must flee from Russia—now, at once. You are going to Germany alone, to-morrow night. Take me with you—take me with—you!"

An irritated look came over Velasco's face. Was the creature mad? "That is nonsense," he said, "I can't take any one with me, and I wouldn't if I could. Besides there is only one passport."

The woman put her hand to her breast. It was throbbing

Olive M. Briggs

madly under the cloak. "You could take—your—wife," she whispered, "Your wife. No one would suspect."

"Really, my dear Madame!"

Velasco yawned behind his palm. "What you say is simply absurd. I tell you I have no wife."

She stretched out her hands to him: "You are a Pole, a Pole!" Her voice rose passionately. "Surely you have suffered; you hate Russia, this cruel, wicked, tyrannous government. Your sympathy is with us, the people, the Liberals, who are trying—oh, I tell you—I must go, at once! After tomorrow it is death, don't you understand,—death? What is it to you, the matter of another passport? You are Velasco?—Every one knows that name, every one. Your wife goes with you to Germany. Oh, take me—take me—I beseech you."

The Violinist stared down at the hooded face. Her voice was tense and vibrating like the tones of an instrument. It moved him strangely. He felt a curious numbness in his throat and a wave passed over him like a chill. She went on, her hands wrung together under the cloak:

"It isn't much I ask. The journey together—at the frontier we part—part forever. The marriage, oh listen—that is nothing, a ceremony, a farce, just a certificate to show the police—the police—"

Her voice died away in a whisper, broken, panting. She fell back against the door, bracing herself against it, gazing up into his eyes.

Velasco stood motionless for a moment; then he turned on his heel and strode over to the fire-place, staring down into the coals. The sight of that bent and shrinking figure, a woman, old and feeble, trembling like a creature hunted, unmanned him.

"I can't do it," he said slowly, "Don't ask me. I am a musician. I have no interest in politics. There is too much risk. I can't, Madame, I can't."

He felt her coming towards him. The flutter of her cloak, it touched him, and her step was light, like a bird limping.

"You read it?" she whispered, "I saw you at the Mariinski; and there—there are the violets on the table, by the violin. Have you forgotten?"

Velasco started: "Who are you?" he exclaimed. "Not Kaya!" He wheeled around and faced her savagely: "You Kaya, never! Was it you who threw the violets—you?"

His dark eyes measured the shrinking form, bent and crippled, shrouded; and he cried out in his disappointment like a peevish boy: "I thought it was she—she! Kaya was young, fair, her face was like a flower; her hair was like gold; her lips were parted, arched and sweet; her eyes—You, you are not Kaya!—Never!"

His voice was angry and full of scorn: "It was all a dream, a mistake. Go—out of my sight; begone! I'll have nothing to do with anarchists."

He snatched the violets from the table and flung them on the hearth: "Begone, or I'll call the police." He was in a tempest of rage. His disappointment rose in his throat and choked him.

The old woman shrank back from him step by step. He followed threateningly:

"Begone, you beggar."

His heart beat unpleasantly. Devil take the old woman! Impostor! She was old and ugly as sin. He was sleepy and weary. Why had he taken the violets; why had he read the note? If the girl were not Kaya, then who—who?

"Come," he cried sharply, "Be off!"

Suddenly the woman buried her head in her hands. She began to sob in long drawn breaths; they shook her form. She fell back against the Erard, trembling and sobbing.

Velasco stared down at her. His anger left him like a flash and his heart softened. Poor thing, poor creature! She was old and feeble, and crippled. He had forgotten. He had only thought of her, Kaya, the girl with the flower-like face. He shook himself, as if out of a dream, and his hand patted the woman's shoulder soothingly. His voice lost its sharpness.

"Don't," he said, "Don't cry like that, my dear Madame—no, don't! It will be all right. I was hasty. Don't mind what I said,—don't—no!"

She dashed his hand from her shoulder and broke into passionate weeping: "You play like a god," she cried, "but you are not; you are a brute. You have no heart. It is your violin that has the heart. Don't touch me—let me go! It was so little I asked, so little!"

She struggled away from him, but Velasco pursued her. His heart misgave him. He grasped her cloak with one hand, the hood with the other, trying to raise it; "Stop!" he said, "I can't stand a woman crying, young or old. I can't stand it; it makes me sick. Stop, I tell you! I'll do anything. I'll—I'll marry you—You shall go to Germany with me. Only stop for heaven's sake. Don't cry like that—don't!"

He stooped over the shrinking figure still lower; his arm pressed her shoulder. She struggled with him blindly, still sobbing.

"Now, by heaven," cried Velasco, "If you are to be my wife, I'll see your face at least. Be still, Madame, be still!"

The woman cowered away from him, holding out her hands, pressing him back. "I beg of you—I beseech you," she said, "Not my face! No—no, Monsieur!"

She gazed at him in terror, and as she gazed, the hood slipped back from her hair; it fell in a golden flood to her shoulders, curling in little rings and waves about her forehead, her neck; veiling her face. She gave a cry.

Velasco stood for a moment petrified, staring down into the frightened eyes that were like twin wells of blue fixed on his own. Then he leaped forward, snatched at the cloak, flung out his arms,—he had clasped the air. She was gone. The door slammed back in his face and the sound of her hurrying footsteps, light as a bird's, fled in the distance.

He was all alone in the room.

Velasco rubbed his eyes with his hand and stared about him, strangely, mechanically, like a sleep-walker. "What a dream! Ye gods, what a dream!" He stretched his limbs yawning and laughed aloud; then he paled suddenly. Was it a dream; or no—impossible. On the sleeve of his black velvet jacket something glistened and sparkled, a thread as of gold, fine and slender like silk, invisible almost as the fibrous strings of his bow.

Olive M. Briggs

He raised it between his fingers. Then slowly, heavily, he went back to his seat before the fire-place and flung himself down.

The lamp-light fell on the Persian rug dimly, flickeringly, the colours were soft as an ancient fresco; the jewels were gone, and the coals burned lower, dying. He lit a cigarette and began to smoke. The violin was in his arms. He played low to himself, dreamily, fitfully, his eyes half closed, dark slits beneath the brows.

At his feet lay the violets crushed and strewn; a twist of paper creased, blotted.

The light of the lamp grew dimmer. The malachite clock struck again and again. The night passed.

CHAPTER IV

Below the Nicholai Bridge, on the right quay of the Neva, stands the palace of the Grand-Duke Stepan, a huge, granite structure, massive in form and splendid in architecture.

The palace was ablaze with light. In the famous ball-room thousands of electric bulbs twinkled and sparkled, star-shaped and dazzling. Its lofty, dome-like vault, resting on marble columns, was encircled by a balcony, narrow and sculptured, from which the music of the band rose and fell, soft, entrancing, invisible, as from the clouds. The walls were of reddish marble rounded at the corners. The floor, shining, polished as a mirror, reflected the swaying forms of the dancers as they whirled to and fro.

Beyond, on the grand stair-case, the guests ascended slowly in groups of twos and threes, flecking the marble with splashes of colour, radiant, vivid, like clusters of rose leaves strewn on the steps. The perfume was intoxicating, languorous. Light trills as of laughter and snatches of talk, gay and fleeting, mingled with the rhythm of the violins.

The ball was at its height.

In an arch of the stair-case stood a young officer. He was leaning nonchalantly against the carved balustrade; the

scarlet and gold of his uniform shone against a green back-
ground of palms, distinguishing his broad shoulders from
among the rest. The palms screened him as in a niche.

The officer was swarthy of complexion with a short, black
mustache, and his eyes, small and near together, roamed
carelessly over the throng. As the groups approached the
head of the stair-case, one after the other, he saluted smiling,
half heeding, and his eyes roved on still more carelessly;
sometimes they crossed.

Whenever they crossed, his eyes would remain fixed, intent,
for a moment, on some one advancing to the foot of the stair-
case, eagerly watching as the form came nearer and nearer.
Then the muscles relaxed. He frowned impatiently, tapping
his sword against the carvings.

"Hiss-s-t—Prince Michel!"

The whisper came from behind the leaves of the palms and
they swayed slightly, trembling as from a movement, or a
breath.

The officer started, turning his black eyes swiftly, fiercely on
the green, and then looked away again.

"Ha, Boris!" he muttered, hardly moving his lips, "How you
come creeping behind one!—What is it, a message?"

"Hist-st! Speak low."

The voice was like the faint murmur of crickets on a hot
summer's day. "The Duke has gone."

"Gone? What! The devil he has!"

"Sh-h!—not five minutes ago! A message came from the Tsar himself. He has just slipped away."

The officer gazed straight ahead of him smiling, and bowed to a couple ascending the stair-case. His lips parted as if in greeting. "Did he send you to tell me?"

"No, the Duchess. She has made some excuse and is receiving alone. No one suspects, not yet; but the guests must be diverted, or else—"

"Be still, Boris, be still, you shake the leaves like a bull. When will he return?"

"By midnight, Prince. Could you start the mazurka at once?"

"Presently, Boris. Go and tell my mother I will—presently. The Countess is late, unaccountably late! Is the snow heavy to-night on the quay; are the sledges blocked? Hiss-st!— There she comes!"

The trembling of the leaves ceased suddenly and the young officer leaned forward, his sword clanking, his eyes crossed and fixed on a vague white spot in the distant foyer.

"She is coming! How slowly she moves! What a throng!— There, she comes, white and sweet like a lily, a flower!" The Prince waved his hand; his sword clanked again. "No, she doesn't see me; her eyes are on the ground—and her hair, it gleams like a crown."

The two figures climbing the grand marble stair-case moved forward slowly, step by step, mingling with the flash and colour of the crowd, lost for a moment at the bend, then reappearing again. The man, evidently a general, was magnificent in his uniform; his breast regal with orders and

Olive M. Briggs

medals, his grey head held high and his form stiff and straight. On his arm was the Countess, his daughter.

She clung to him, her lips were smiling and her white robes trailed the marble behind her. She was like a young queen, charming and gracious, bowing to right and to left. As the groups drew aside to let her pass, they whispered together, looking up at the carved balustrade; then the crowd closed again.

At the top of the stair-case the Prince sprang forward. He greeted the General hastily, saluting. Then the watchers behind saw how the Countess paused, hesitated, and then, at a few whispered words from the Prince, placed her hand on his arm and the two young figures, the white and the scarlet, disappeared within the doorway.

The violins rose and fell in a dreamy measure. From the sculptured gallery the sound came mysterious, enchanting, swaying the feet with the force of its rhythm.

"Not to-night," said the Countess, "No!" She drew herself away from the arm of the Prince and her lashes drooped over her eyes. "I am tired—later perhaps, Prince."

Her voice, low and remonstrating, was lost in the swing of the waltz. With a sudden, swift movement the scarlet and white seemed welded together, whirling into the vortex of light and of motion.

No word was exchanged. They whirled, gliding, twisting in and out among the dancers; and suddenly, swiftly, as at a signal, the music broke into the measure of the mazurka. A cry went up from the throng. In a twinkling the floor was cleared, the crowd pressed back against the columns; under the reddish marble of the dome four couples gathered, poised hand in hand.

The uniforms of the officers glowed in the light, rich and scarlet, faced with silver and gold. The gowns of their partners were brocade and velvet, purple and crimson, lilac and pearl. Then from the balcony, high up, unseen, the rhythm changed again like a flash, and with it the national dance began.

At first the movements were slow, the steps graceful; the feet seemed scarcely to move, barely gliding over the floor. One by one the couples retreated, the last left alone; and then interchanging. The music grew faster. In that moment, when they were left alone, the Prince bent his head to the slim, swaying whiteness by his side:

"Why did you come so late?" he whispered, "Where were you?"

The Countess' hand was cold like ice. She drew it away and danced on; then she whispered back:

"The Duke! Where is he to-night? He is not here! Why is the mazurka so early, tell me."

They interchanged again.

"Hush," said the Prince, "You noticed?—Don't speak. He has gone to the Tsar.—What is it? Are you ill?"

"He has—gone?"

"Dance, Countess, dance. Don't stop; are you mad? Come nearer. Hush!—The Tsar sent for him, but he will be back at midnight. No one must know."

The figure of the mazurka grew stranger and more compli-
cated. When they were thrown together again, the Countess
lifted her blue eyes to the eyes of the Prince. They seemed to
look at her and yet to look past her; they were crossed. She
shivered slightly and turned her head. Her white figure,
slender and light as thistledown, floated away from him, and
then in a moment she was back, their hands had touched;
they were whirling together faster and faster, the tips of her
slippers scarcely touching the floor. She closed her eyes.

"You won't tell, not a soul, I can trust you?" whispered the
Prince. "Come closer, closer. There is a plot to-night. Boris
told me. The Secret Service men are everywhere, watching.
Don't be frightened, Countess—your hand is so cold. Can
you hear me? Bend your head—so! They hope to make
arrests before he returns."

"When—when does he return?"

"Sh—h! At midnight. Dance faster, faster—Let yourself go!"

The music broke into a mad riot of rhythm; the violins
seemed to run races with one another in an intoxication of
sound, pulsing, penetrating, overpowering. The white figure
twirled in the Prince's arms, her gold hair a blot against the
scarlet of his sleeve, faster and faster. Her head drooped; her
eyes closed again.

The rhythm was alive, tempting, subtle, like a madness in the
veins; and as they whirled, the rubato, dreamy, sudden,
caught them as in a leash; the steps faltered, slower, more
lingering; slower, still slower until the music stopped, dying
away into the dome of the vault in a last faint echo of sound.

The Countess swayed suddenly.

Her face was white as the lace on her bosom, and her eyes grew dark and big, with black shadows sweeping her cheeks. Others stepped forward to the dance; their places were filled and the music commenced again.

"Lean on me," whispered the Prince, "Are you ill? Countess, lean on my arm—so."

His voice was hoarse and excited. He was swaying a little himself from the intoxication of the dance.

"Take me away somewhere, some quiet place," she whispered back. "Let me rest—I am faint."

He drew her after him and the two figures, the scarlet and the white, passed under the archway into a salon beyond. The Prince raised a curtain: "This is the Duke's own room," he said in her ear, "Go under—be quick!"

The curtain fell heavily behind them and the two stood alone in the Grand-Duke's room. There was a desk in the corner littered with papers, a lamp stood beside, heavily shaded, and back in the shadowy recesses was a couch.

"Help me there," whispered the Countess, "And then go—go, Prince, leave me. My head is on fire! See, my cheeks, my hands, how they burn? Help me to the couch."

She staggered and almost fell as they approached it, burying her face in her hands.

"I can't leave you," said the Prince. He was on his knees beside her, kissing her hands, trying to draw them down from her face. "Kaya, what is the matter? Don't hide your eyes—look at me. Shall I call some one? Are you ill?"

Olive M. Briggs

The Countess drew back against the cushions, shuddering, pushing him from her: "Don't call any one," she said, "Give me that water on the table there." Her eyes were wide open now and dilated; the hair fell disordered in golden rings and waves about the oval of her face. She drew her breath heavily; her bosom rising and falling like waves after a storm. One hand pressed her lace as if to clutch the pulsing and steady it; the other held the glass to her trembling lips.

The Prince hovered over the couch. He was pale and the crossing of his eyes was more pronounced than ever. "Drink now," he whispered soothingly as if to a child in trouble, "Drink it slowly. It is wine, not water, and will bring back your strength. It was the dance; ah, it was so fast, so mad. You were wonderful! The blood beats in my veins still; I can feel the rhythm throbbing, can you? Speak to me, Countess—are you better?"

"Is any one here," said the girl faintly, "Are we alone?"

"Yes, yes, we are alone."

"Will the Duke come in?"

"Not yet. Put your head back against the cushions and rest. The colour is gone from your cheeks and you are pale like a broken flower. Listen—do you hear the violins in the distance? Your feet move like mine; every pulse in your body is tingling and throbbing. Rest; don't speak, and in a moment—Kaya—"

Again the Countess pushed him back, her blue eyes sparkling, flashing on his: "Prince, hush! Don't speak to me like that. You don't know, how can you! Poor boy—poor boy! Don't look at me; I tell you, don't look at me. In the dusk it might be the Duke himself, his very self! Go—Leave me a little. If he were good like you—but you will be bad too when you are older, wicked, cruel—the blood is there in your veins. You will be like the rest. Keep away from me, Michel. Don't kiss my hands, not—my—hands!"

The Countess tore them away and gazed at the young officer, her eyes wild and dilated. She gave a little cry as of pain.

"No—no! I can bear all the rest, but not this—not this! Get up off your knees Prince. Leave me—leave me for a little while—I must think; I must be alone and think."

Her hair sparkled and gleamed against the cushions. One hand was still clasped to her breast. He stooped over her, panting.

"Come and dance with me, Kaya—dearest. You are well now; your cheeks are like roses. The wine is so strong when one is giddy. Let me put my arms about you—come! I love you. Ah, your hair is like a halo; your lips are trembling. The tears in your eyes are like dew, Kaya."

The Countess rose slowly to her feet. "Yes, you are like your father already," she cried, "Already you are cowardly. You are strong and you think I am weak." Her head was thrown back; she measured him scornfully, "Go and dance, sir. Leave me, I tell you."

The Prince held out his hands. "Leave you!" he cried, "No, Kaya, no. Come and dance."

"Leave me—leave me."

He came nearer: "Are you still faint? Will you rest and let me come back? When? How soon?"

Olive M. Briggs

"Leave me."

He took out his watch: "Nearly midnight," he cried, "then the Duke will return. When the clock strikes, Kaya, it will be our dance. You will waltz with me then—once more? As soon as the clock strikes?"

"Leave me."

"A quarter of an hour, Kaya, no more? I will send word to Boris. He will guard the curtain so no one will enter, unless it is the Duke himself. As soon as the clock strikes, you promise, we will waltz together?"

"Go, Michel, go—I promise."

The Prince made a step forward as though to gather the shrinking figure in his arms. He hesitated; then he moved towards the curtain; hesitated again and looked behind him. Then the heavy folds fell and the girl was alone.

She stood for a moment, watching the folds, then she put her hands to her eyes and swayed as though she were falling.

"God!" she cried, "Must I do it? Is there no other—no other instrument?" She sobbed to herself in little broken words, catching her breath: "*I vow—I vow—without weakness, or hesitation, or mercy—with mine own hands if—needs be.*"

She staggered forward, still sobbing, and bent over the desk. Something white fluttered and fell from her lace; she smoothed it with her fingers; gazed at it.

"God!" she cried, "Oh, God!"

Then she clasped her breast again and drew something out,

something dark and hard. She gave a startled glance about the room, covering it with her arms; her form shivering as though in a chill.

"In the name of the Black Cross I swear—I swear—"

Then she crept back to the couch and sank on the floor behind it, covering her face with her hands. As she did so, the door on the corridor opened a crack, then wider, slowly wider, and some one came in. The form was that of a man. He looked about him. The room was still, deserted, and he gave a sigh of relief, hurrying over to the desk. When he turned up the lamp, the light revealed a bundle of papers which he laid on the desk, examining them one after the other, putting his face close to the lamp, studying, absorbed.

The face was that of the Grand-Duke Stepan; his beaked nose, his grey, upturned mustache, his eyes small and crossed. They were fixed on the sheets. All of a sudden he started violently.

Beside him on the desk, just under the lamp, was a slip of paper. There was nothing on the paper but a Black Cross graven, above it: *Смертb*.

As the Duke gazed at it, his face grew ashen, his mouth twitched, his eyes seemed fairly to start from his head; his knees knocked together. He glanced fearfully around, trying vainly to steady his hands.

"Without weakness, without hesitation, or mercy, by mine own hands if needs be, I swear—"

Was it a voice shrieking in his ears? He cowered backwards, huddled together, shivering.

Olive M. Briggs

"*I swear—*"

Suddenly there came the click of a revolver. A shot rang out; a moan. The Duke stood motionless for a second; then he faltered, twisted and fell on his face with his arms outstretched.

CHAPTER V

It was snowing steadily. The drops came so thick and so fast that the city was shrouded as in a great white veil, falling from the sky to the earth. Drifts were piled in the streets; they were frozen and padded as with a carpet, and the sound of sleigh-bells rang muffled in the distance. It was night and dark, with a bitter wind that came shrieking about the corners, blowing the snow, as it fell, into a riot of feathery flakes; sudden gusts that raided the drifts, driving the white maze hither and thither, flinging it up and away in a very fury of madness. The cold was intense.

Before the door of a house on the little Morskaia stood a kareta. It was large and covered. Behind and on top several boxes were strapped, protected from the snow by wrappings of oil-cloth, and on the driver's seat was a valise.

The horses pawed the snow impatiently, tossing their heads and snorting whenever the icy blast struck them. The wind was sharp like a whip. Occasionally the kareta made a sudden lurch forward; then, with guttural oaths and excla-mations, the animals were reined back on their haunches, slipping and sliding on the ice, plunging and foaming. The foam turned to ice as it fell, flecking their bits. The breath from their nostrils floated out like a vapour, slender and hoary.

The driver, muffled in furs, swung his arms against his breast, biting his fingers, stamping his feet to keep them from freezing. The kareta, the driver and the horses were covered with snow, lashed by it, blinded with it. They waited wearily. From time to time the driver glanced up at the door of the house and then back at the carriage, shaking his head and muttering fiercely:

"Stand still, you sons of the devil, stand still! You prance and shy as if Satan himself had stuck a dart in you! Hey, there!— Back, back, you limb! Will the Barin never come?"

He swore vigorously to himself under his beard, and the flakes fell from him in a shower. After a while the door of the house opened; some one appeared on the steps and a voice called out:

"Bobo, eh Bobo! Is that you, are you ready? Heavens, what a night!"

"All ready, Monsieur Velasco, all ready."

"The boxes on?"

"Yes, Barin."

"You took my valise, did you?"

"Yes, Barin."

The figure disappeared for an instant within the doorway and the light went out; then he reappeared, carrying a violin-case under his arm, which he screened from the wet with the folds of his cloak, carefully, as a mother would cover the face of her child. He leaped to the carriage.

"All right, Bobo, go ahead. Wait a moment until I get the latch open. Ye gods! I never felt such cold. My fingers are like frozen sticks. There! Now, the Station: Warchavski Voksal—as fast as you can! Ugh, what a storm!"

The Violinist flung himself back in the corner of the kareta, huddling himself in the furs; the windows were shut and his breath made a steam against the panes. The carriage was black as a cave.

"There ought to be another fur!" he said angrily to himself. His teeth were chattering and his whole body shivered against the cushions. "I told Bobo to put in an extra fur. The devil now, where can it be?"

He groped with his hands, feeling the seat beside him, when all of a sudden he gave an exclamation, alarmed, half suppressed, his eyes staring into the darkness, trying vainly to penetrate.

What was it? Something was there, moving, breathing, alive, on the seat close beside him. Gracious heaven! He wasn't alone! Velasco crouched back instinctively, putting out both hands as if to ward off a blow. He listened, peering. Surely something breathed—there, in the corner! He could make out a shadow, an outline.—No, nothing—it was nothing at all.

His pulses beat rapidly; he groped again with his hands, slowly, fearfully, hesitating and then groping again. It was as though something, someone were trying to elude him in the darkness. His breath came fast; he listened again.

Something cowered and breathed—"Bozhe moi!" He gripped his lip with his teeth and hurled himself forward, grappling into the furthermost recesses of the kareta. His hands grasped a cloak, a human shoulder, a body. It dragged away from

Olive M. Briggs

him. He clutched it and something shrank back into the shadows. His eyes were blind; he could see nothing, he could hear nothing; he could only feel. It was breathing.

His hand moved cautiously over the cloak, the shoulder. It resisted him, trying vainly to escape; and then, as the carriage dashed on through the darkness, he dragged the thing forward, nearer—nearer, struggling. The breath was on his cheeks. He felt it distinctly—the rustle of something alive.

Velasco clenched his teeth together, clutching the thing, and held it under the window-pane, close, close, straining forward. As he did so the rays of a street lamp fell through the glass, a faint, pale light through the steam on the panes; a flash and it was over. Velasco gave a cry.

Beside him was a woman, slight and veiled, and she was crouching away from him, holding her hands before her face, panting, frightened, even as he was.

"Who are you?" cried Velasco, "What are you? Speak, for the love of heaven! I feel as if I were going mad. Speak!"

He shook the cloak in his trembling grasp and, as he did so, a hand pressed into his own. It was bare, and soft like the leaf of a rose. He grasped it. The fingers clung to him, alive and warm. Velasco hesitated. Then he dropped the hand and from his pocket he snatched a match, striking it against the side of the carriage. It sputtered and went out. He struck another. It flickered for a moment and he held it between his hands, coaxing it. It burned and he held it out, gazing into the corner, coming nearer and nearer. The eyes gleamed at him from behind the veil; nearer—He could see the oval of the face, the lips. Then the match went out.

"Kaya—Kaya!"

He snatched at her hand again in the darkness and held it under the fur. "You came after all," he whispered hoarsely, "I thought I had dreamed it. Speak to me; let me hear your voice."

He felt her bending towards him; her shoulder touched his. "You promised—I hold you to your promise."

"Yes; yes!"

"Have you changed your mind?"

"No.—Don't take your hand away. No! It is horrible, the storm and the blackness. Hear the wind shriek! The hoofs of the horses are padded with snow; they are galloping. How the carriage lurches and sways! Are you afraid, Kaya? Don't—don't take your hand away."

Velasco's voice was husky and forced like a string out of tune. It was strange, extraordinary to be sitting there in that dark, black cave, his hand clasping the hand of a woman, a stranger. The two sat silent. The horses plunged forward.

Suddenly they stopped. Velasco started as out of a dream and sprang to the window, wiping the steam from the panes with his sleeve.

"Bobo!" he cried, "Madman! This is not the Station. Where are you going, idiot—fool!"

His voice was smothered suddenly by a hand across his lips.

"Hush, Monsieur, have you forgotten? The driver knows, he is one of us. Come with me; and I pray you, I beseech you, don't speak, don't make a sound; step softly and follow."

In a moment the girl was out of the carriage and Velasco behind. Her veil fluttered back; her cloak brushed his shoulder. The storm and the wind beat against them. He ran blindly forward, battling with the gale; but fast as he went she went faster. He could scarcely keep up. In the distance behind them, the carriage and horses were lost in a white mist, a whirl.

"Here," she cried, "Bow your head, quick, the arch—and then through the gate—run! Take my hand in the court—let me lead you. I know every step. Run—run! You waited so long; we shall be late. There is barely time before the train. Ah, run, Monsieur—run!"

The two figures dashed through the alley and into an open cloister, running with their heads bowed against the wind, struggling with the snow in their eyes, in their throats; blinded, panting.

"Stop!" gasped Velasco, "I can't run like this. Stop! You mad thing, you witch! Where, where are you going? Stop, I tell you!"

She dragged at his hand. "Come—a moment further. Come, Monsieur. Ah, it is death—don't falter. Run!"

She caught at a little door under the wall and pushed it madly. It yielded. He sprang in behind her; and then he stood blinking, amazed.

They were alone in the dark, ghostly nave of a huge Church. The long rows of columns stretched out in the distance, tall and stately like pines in a forest; the aisles were broad and shadowy, leading far off in a distant perspective to the outline of an altar and a high cross suspended. They were dim, barely visible.

"Where are we?" he murmured, faltering. "Kaya, speak—tell me."

She put up her face close to his and he saw that her lips were quivering, her eyes blurred with tears. Her veil was white with the snow, like a bride's. She dragged at his hand, and he followed her dumbly, their footsteps echoing, a soft patter across the marble of the church.

It was absolutely dark; only on the far distant altar three candles were lighted, three sparks, red and restless, like fire-flies gleaming. Otherwise the nave, the chancel, the transepts were as one vast blackness stretching before them. They fled on in silence; their goal was the candles.

At first the space before the altar seemed empty, deserted, like the rest of the Church; but as they approached, nearer and nearer, three forms seemed to melt from the back of the choir and stood on the steps; two were figures in cloaks; the third was a priest. His surplice shone in the shadows against the outline of the columns. He mounted the steps of the altar and stood with his face to the cross. They seemed to be waiting.

To Velasco the sound of his footsteps echoed and rever-berated on the marble, filling the darkness. The noise of them was terrible. He would have covered his ears with his hands, but the girl urged him forward. The soft fingers crept about his own like a vine, clinging, irresistible.

"Come," she breathed, "ah, come, Monsieur—come!"

Then he followed, moving forward hurriedly, blindly, like

Olive M. Briggs

one hypnotized. His senses were dulled; his will was inert. When he came to himself he was kneeling beside her on the marble, and he heard the voice of the priest, chanting slowly in Slavonic:

"Blessed is our God always, and ever, and unto ages of ages.

"In peace let us pray to the Lord for the servant of God, Velasco, and for the hand-maid of God, Kaya, who now plight each other their troth, and for their salvation. . . . That he will send down upon them perfect and peaceful love. . . . That he will preserve them in oneness of mind and in steadfastness of faith. . . . That he will bless them with a blameless life. . . . That he will deliver us from all tribulation, wrath, peril and necessity. . . . Lord have mercy!

"Lord have mercy!"

He listened in bewilderment; was it himself, or his ghost, his shadow. He tried to think, but everything melted before him in a mist. The girl by his side was a wraith; they were dead, and this was some strange unaccountable happening in another world. The marble felt cold to his knees. Velasco tried to move, to rise, but the hand of the priest held him down. The voice chanted on:

"Hast thou, Velasco, a good, free and unconstrained will and a firm intention to take unto thyself to wife this woman, Kaya, whom thou seest here before thee?"

And in the pause, he heard himself answering, strangely, dreamily, in a voice that was not his own:

"I have, reverend Father."

"Thou hast not promised thyself to any other bride?"

"I have not promised myself, reverend Father."

Then he felt the hand of the priest, pressing the crown down on his forehead; it weighed on his brow, and when he tried to shake it off he could not.

"The servant of God, Velasco, is crowned unto the handmaid of God, Kaya. In the name of the Father, and of the Son, and of the Holy Spirit. Amen."

"The servant of God, Kaya, is crowned unto the servant of God, Velasco. In the name of the Father, and of the Son, and of the Holy Spirit. Amen."

"O Lord our God, crown them with glory and honour.

"O Lord our God, crown them with glory and honour.

"O Lord our God, crown them with glory and honour!"

Velasco passed his hand over his face; he was breathing heavily. The crown glittered in the darkness.

"And so may the Father and the Son, and the Holy Spirit, the all-holy, consubstantial and life-giving Trinity, one Godhead, and one Kingdom, bless you, and grant you length of days, . . . prosperity of life and faith: and fill you with all abundance of earthly good things, and make you worthy to obtain the blessings of the promise: through the prayers of the holy Birth-giver of God, and of all the saints. Amen."

"Glory to the Father and to the Son and to the Holy Spirit now, and ever, and unto ages and ages."

"Amen."

Olive M. Briggs

The chanting ceased suddenly, and there was silence. Then he felt something falling against him, and he staggered to his feet, dragging the girl up with him. She trembled and shook, pushing him back with her hands; her eyes were full of terror, staring up into his, the eyes of her husband. Again everything grew misty and swayed.

He was signing a paper; how his fingers quivered; he could scarcely hold the pen! The priest drew nearer, and the two cloaked figures. They all signed; and then he felt the paper crackling in the bosom of his coat, where he had thrust it. They were hurrying back through the dark, ghostly nave.

They were running, and the sound of their footsteps seemed louder and noisier than before; they ran side by side, through the door in the wall, the cloisters, the arch, bowing their heads; and there was the carriage, a great blot of whiteness, the horses like spectres. The snow came whirling through the air in sharp, icy flakes, cutting the skin. The wind grew fiercer, more violent.

With a last desperate effort Velasco dashed forward, pursuing the veil, the fluttering cloak—and the door of the carriage closed behind them. In that moment, as it closed, the horses leaped together, as twin bullets from the mouth of a cannon; galloping, lashed and terrified through the night. It was still inside the kareta.

Suddenly Velasco was conscious of a voice at his elbow, whispering to him out of the silence: "Thank you, Monsieur, ah, I thank you! We shall be at the station directly; then a few hours more and it will be—over! You will never see— me—again! I thank you—I thank you with all my heart."

The voice was soft and low, like a violin when the mute is on the strings. He could scarcely hear it for the lurching of the carriage. The horses gave a final plunge forward, and then fell back suddenly, reined in by an iron hand, and the kareta came to a standstill.

The station was all light and confusion; porters were rushing about, truckmen and officials, workmen carrying coloured lanterns. "Not a second to spare!" cried Velasco, "Send the trunks after me, Bobo—Here—my valise!"

He snatched up his violin-case, and the slim, dark-veiled figure darted beside him. "If we miss it!" he heard her crying in his ear, "I shall never forgive myself! I shall—never—forgive myself!"

"We shan't miss it!" cried Velasco, "I have the tickets, the passports for you and for me! Here—to the left! The doors are still open!"

An official rushed forward and took the valise from Velasco's hand: "Here, sir—here! First class compartment!"

Velasco nodded breathlessly, and the two sank down on the crimson cushions; the door slammed. "Ye gods!" They were alone in the compartment; they were saved! Velasco gave a little laugh of triumph. He was hugging his violin close in his arms, and opposite him sat the slim veiled figure. She was looking at him from behind the veil—and she was his wife. "Ye gods!" he laughed again.

"Why are you trembling?" he said, "We are safe now. I told you I had the passports. Are you cold, or afraid?—You shake like a leaf!"

The girl put out her hand, touching his. "Did you see?" she breathed, "There—on the platform—Boris, the Chief of the Third Section!—He was watching!"

Olive M. Briggs

Velasco laughed again aloud, happily, like a boy: "What of it? Let him watch! Put up your veil, Kaya. Great heavens, what a night it has been! My heart is going still like a hammer—is yours? Lean back on the cushions—put up your veil. Let me see you once,—let me see you! Look at me as you did in the Theatre—Kaya! Don't tremble."

"He is there," breathed the girl, "I see him behind the curtain! He is talking to the official—The train is late and it doesn't start. Why doesn't it start?"

She gave a little moan and peered out through the veil: "Something has happened, Monsieur! The officials are clustered together, talking—there is some excitement! They are gesticulating and several are pointing to the train! What is it—what is it?"

Velasco laughed again; but the laugh died in his throat. The two turned and gazed at one another with wide, frightened eyes.

"The Chief of the Third Section—see! He is going from compartment to compartment—He is looking at the passports! He is coming here—here!"

CHAPTER VI

"Your passports, Monsieur—Madame?"

Velasco thrust his hand slowly into the breast pocket of his coat and drew out the precious papers. His manner was cold and indifferent, and his eyes had narrowed into sleepy slits again beneath the heaviness of his brows.

Kaya was leaning back on the cushions with the veil drawn closely over her face. She was tapping the panels of the door with a dainty, nervous foot. Neither glanced at the official.

The Chief of the Third Section was in evening dress with a fur cloak thrown hastily over his shoulders. He would have passed for an ordinary citizen on his way to a ball if it had not been for the strangeness of such an attire in a railway station, and the cluster of anxious, humble officials bowing and gesticulating about him. The Chief examined the passports closely and at some length; then he tossed an order over his shoulder in a quick, sharp tone to the group of officials, and one hurried away.

"This lady, Monsieur, she is your wife?"

The voice of the Chief, as he turned to Velasco, was like the passing of a brush over wool. The Violinist shuddered.

"Certainly sir, she is my wife," he returned curtly. "It is so stated on the paper, I believe."

"It is," said the Chief, "The writing is plain, quite clear. Will you be good enough to raise your veil, Madame?"

Kaya shrank back. "My veil!" she stammered. She half rose from her seat, supporting herself, with her hands pressed down on the cushions, gazing up at the waiting official. "No—my veil!—What do you mean?"

"I am sorry to trouble you," said the Chief sharply, "but I said: 'your veil.' Kindly raise it at once. Ha!—Why shouldn't you show your face, Madame?"

His burly form filled the doorway and the white of his shirt front, half screened by the fur, gleamed under the electric light. He seemed enormous.

Velasco's brows lifted suddenly until his eyes were wide open and blazing: "Stand back, you impudent scoundrel!" he cried, "Stand away from my wife! How dare you?"

"Come!" said the Chief. His voice was still sharper. "No nonsense, Monsieur. The veil must be raised and immediately; you are keeping the whole train back. What do you suppose I am here for?" There was menace in his tone as he took a step forward. "Now, Madame, will you raise it, or shall I?"

Kaya retreated slowly to the farther side of the compartment. "Stop," she whispered to Velasco. "Don't get angry; don't do anything, it is useless. Come back in the shadow."

Then she turned and faced the official defiantly, throwing up the veil. Her face was very pale, her eyes were blue and dark, like two pools without a bottom, and her lips pressed together, quivering slightly. Velasco stared at her for a moment and drew a step nearer, laying his hand on her shoulder. He was trembling with rage.

"Are you satisfied now, you cur?" he cried, "Look at her then. You will never see another face as beautiful, not in the whole length and breadth of your cursed country. Look— while you have the chance! By heaven, whoever you are, chief of the devil himself, I'll report you for this—I'll—"

A shrill whistle cut through the torrent of words, and in another moment the Chief had stepped back, and the under officials came crowding through the door of the compartment.

"Arrest them both," cried the Chief shortly, "Get them away at once and don't let them out of your hands. 'Peter and Paul,' quick! The woman is—" He whispered something hoarsely.

In a second the two were surrounded, their hands were chained; they were bound like sheep and dragged, first one, then the other, to a covered sleigh at the rear of the station.

"Put them in—hurry!" cried the Chief, "Gag the fellow; don't let him speak! Is the woman secure, so she can't scream, or moan? Take them off!"

The sleigh started, and the two lay side by side on the floor, jostled by the lurching of the runners, their flesh cut and bruised by the ropes, their mouths parched and panting behind the gags. They could not stir, or moan, or make a sign. They were helpless.

When the sleigh stopped in the grim inner court of the fortress, they were carried out into the darkness, and borne

Olive M. Briggs

like animals through long, damp passages, down innumerable steps and dim windings until finally a door clicked and opened. They were thrust inside, their bindings were cut, and the door clicked again, slamming in its socket with the sickening crash of steel against steel; the sound reverberating hard and metallic like a blow against the eardrum, finally dying away in the distance, echo upon echo until all was silent.

The girl lay still on the floor where they had left her. She had swooned, and as she returned to consciousness slowly, gradually, her breath came in little gasps through her parted lips and she moaned as she lay. Velasco had dragged himself to his knees and was peering about him, feeling with his hands in the dim waning light. He was muttering to himself in little outbursts of anger and rebellion, rocking his arms to and fro.

"What a hole! What a beastly place! The floor is wet; ugh!—The walls are dank and shiny—things are crawling! Good heavens, something ran over my foot!—It must be a rat, scurrying—scampering! Sapristi! There's another! What a scrape to be in—what a scrape!"

The girl lifted her head and looked at him, straining her eyes for the outline of his shoulders, the mass of his dark curls. He had turned half away and was wringing his hands, feeling them and exclaiming to himself. She crept towards him and stretched out her hand, touching his shoulder.

"Monsieur—Ah, Monsieur Velasco!"

He shuddered away from her: "You, is it you! Are you alive? I thought you were dead! Mon Dieu, I thought I was shut in with a corpse! It is frightful, horrible! I have suffered! God, how I have suffered—the torture of the damned!"

"Monsieur!"

"My hands are cut; I know they are cut! Look, can you see, —are they covered with blood? I am sure I feel it trickling! —Look!"

"No—no, Monsieur, there is no blood."

"I tell you I feel it—and my shoulder, my arm—I shall never be able to play again! I am ruined—ruined—and for what? Why did you come to me? Why didn't you go to someone else—anybody?"

"Ah forgive me, forgive me." The girl crept closer and laid her hand on his shoulder, pathetically as if half afraid. "I shouldn't have gone to you, but—listen, Monsieur—let me tell you—let me explain! I thought there was no danger, not for you, otherwise—Oh, do believe me, not for the world would I have done it! I knew you were an artist; Bobo told us you were going to Germany—I thought—Can you ever forgive me?"

Her voice broke a little and she was silent.

Velasco went on rocking himself, feeling his arms, his hands, his fingers at intervals. "Don't talk," he said, "You make me nervous. You did very wrong; you ought never to have come to me. I hate anarchists; I never could bear them; and now they take me for one! I shall live here all my days— and my Stradivarius, my treasure—Heaven knows where they have put it—lying on the platform of the station, or perhaps broken, or stolen! I shall never see it again, never! Ah, it is cruel—it is not to be borne! Don't speak, I tell you, I can't bear it! You shouldn't have coaxed me!—Ugh! these rats—brr—did you feel it?"

Olive M. Briggs

The girl gave a muffled cry. She had shrunk away in the corner, but now she crouched forward, her eyes dilated, staring into the darkness.

"A rat, Monsieur? Ah, it is so dark—I feel things, crawling—crawling; and the damp oozes down from the walls. I am frightened—frightened!"

The last words were a whisper; her throat swelled and she was choked, trembling with terror. She put out her hand and touched something soft—it slid from her and ran. She cried out faintly.

"Come here," said Velasco, "Come nearer! The rats won't hurt you. Rest on my cloak, poor child, are you cold? Where are you?—Let me touch you!"

"Here," said the girl, "I can feel the edge of your cloak; don't put it around me—no! I deserve to suffer, but you—no wonder you hate me! Don't put it around me."

"Come nearer," said Velasco, "I can't see you in this devilish darkness. Are you crying?"

"No, Monsieur, no, let me tell you—it was your playing, your playing that night. I saw you, and then the thought came to me—I will go to him, he will help me; and then—I came."

"Your teeth click together like a castanet rattling," said Velasco, "You tremble like a string under the bow. Come closer. There—one ran over my sleeve, curse the creature! Did you feel him, the vermin? Put my cloak close around you."

"No—no—not your cloak! You are shivering yourself, you need it. Don't—I pray you!"

There was a moment of silent struggle between them.

"Keep still," said Velasco, "My hands are cut, but they are strong still, and yours are like wax, soft as rose leaves. Hold it around you; don't push it away. Now, lean against me; they won't touch you."

The struggle continued for a moment; then the form of the girl relaxed, her head drooped and he felt the light rings of her hair brushing his cheek. She started and then sank back again.

"Can you hear me?" said Velasco, "Perhaps there are spies, people listening; no one can tell. Put your lips to my ear. Why were we arrested, do you know? What have you done?—Ah, these rats! Make a noise with your feet; scuffle as I do, that will drive them away.—"

"I—I can't tell you," whispered the girl, "No—it was nothing, don't ask me. You will know in the morning."

"Tell me now," said Velasco, "When we talk, the darkness seems less, not so terrible. I like to feel you breathing against me; your form is so little and light. Don't move! Put your fingers in mine now and tell me.—Why won't you tell me?— Speak louder."

The girl trembled and he put his arm closer about her.

"Are you afraid of me?" he said, "My tempers are nothing; they are like a gust and it is over. I didn't mean what I said. When I think of my violin, that it is lost, gone forever perhaps, that my hands are so numb and so stiff, it makes me frantic. I feel as if I should go mad for a moment, locked in here; and I never could bear the dark, never; not when I was a child. I see things; sounds ring in my ears. I want to cry

Olive M. Briggs

out, and storm, and fling myself against the walls; do you? It is my nature, my temperament, I was always like that. My nerves are on fire. Stay by me. When I feel your hand—Kaya, your hair is like silk. Don't move. What was it you did?"

"Only what was just," breathed the girl, "and right. I could not help myself, I could not. I had taken the oath. I was only the instrument."

"The what—?" said Velasco. "If you were an instrument I should take you in my arms and play on you. The strings would be the strands of your hair and my bow would caress them. The tones would be thrilling and soft like your voice; your cheek would be the arch on which my cheek rests. I would shut my eyes and play on you, and you would answer me, and we would sway together, your heart on my breast.—Ah! Where am I? Forgive me, I thought for a moment—Don't be frightened, I thought you were my Stradivarius. I was dreaming.—What were you saying? An instrument—I don't understand."

"Let me go," cried the girl, "don't hold me! Take your cloak from my shoulders. You wouldn't understand if I did tell you. You are an artist and understand nothing but your art. What do you know of the conditions we are struggling against, the suffering, the horrible suffering of our country?"

"Don't be angry," said Velasco, "I talk to my violin sometimes like that. There was nothing to flare up about; I was dreaming, I tell you! What do you know of such things yourself? Ugh! Leave them alone, child; leave all ugly things alone! Come back, or the rats will run over you."

"It is terrible the things that happen," whispered the girl. She was on her knees and she was pushing him away with her hands. "I never knew until lately, but now—now I have met the Revolutionists; they have talked to me, they have told me. They are splendid men. Some of them are extreme, so am I. I hate the Tsar. I loathe him; I loathe them all! I would kill them all if I could."

She was trembling violently: "It is true that I have—" And then she began sobbing, struggling with Velasco as he drew her to him.

"Be still," he said, "Hush! Your voice was like a trumpet then. You are not like a girl at all; you are like a soldier fighting for his flag. What are you talking about? Hush! Let me wrap you again. The rats are getting worse! Creep closer and rest on my arm. The Tsar is the little Father; we must respect him and speak low about him always."

The girl caught her breath, sinking back on his shoulder, wrapped in his fur. She tried to resist him, but his arm was strong and encircled her, his hand clasped her own; it was supple and the wrist was like a hinge. There was a power, an electric force in his touch, a magnetism—she shut her eyes, yielding to it. She was like a violin after all; if he chose to play on her with his bow! Ah—she quivered.

"Monsieur," she said low, "You don't understand. You are a Pole and you care nothing for Poland; how could you understand? And yet you play—my God, how you play, as if you had cared and suffered more than any one in the whole wide world. Have you ever suffered?"

"No," said Velasco, "What should there be to make me suffer? Not until to-night!—Ugh, this is torture, horrible!"

"Have you ever twisted and writhed in an agony of mind that was like madness because—"

Olive M. Briggs

"Of course," said Velasco, "After my concerts I am always like that. It is—" He shuddered. "A black depression creeps over one. Bozhe moi! It is awful! Is that what you mean?"

"No," she said, "that is not what I meant. Tell me, Monsieur, have you ever cared for any one?"

Velasco stretched his cramped limbs and yawned. "Never, any one particularly," he said, "that I can think of. I used to like my old master in Warsaw; and I have friends; good gracious! All over Russia and Germany I have friends. You don't mean that?"

The girl stirred uneasily against his arm.

"Was that another rat?" she said, "I felt something run over my dress."

"Draw the cloak to your chin," whispered Velasco, "Huddle yourself in it. There, are you warm? Put your head down again. One moment you are like a boy ready to fight the universe, the next you shake at the sound of a rat.—Kaya!"

"Yes, Monsieur?"

She shivered, clinging to him.

"What did you say? Say it again; don't tremble like that."

"I would die," she whispered, "A thousand times I would die rather than have brought this on you. If I had known—if I had guessed!"

"Your hair is like down," said Velasco, "a soft, golden fluff. I can't see it, or you; are you there? I shouldn't know if I didn't feel you breathing, and the touch of your head and your hand. Go to sleep; I will watch."

She murmured and stirred in his arms.

"Yes, yes, I forgive you. I never was angry. If only they haven't hurt my violin, my Stradivarius! If they do, I shall drown myself!—But don't think of it; don't speak of it. Be still and sleep."

She murmured again. He laid his cheek to her hair and they sat silent, the girl half unconscious, Velasco staring out into the darkness, his face white and set.

There was a stirring of something within him impossible to fathom; something apart from himself, strange and different, like the birth of a soul; a second personality, unknown, unrevealed. His heavy eyes gleamed through the slits. The round of his chin stiffened; his mouth took new lines. The luxurious artist personality of the musician was dormant for the first time in his life; his virile and masculine side had begun to awaken. The muscles of his arm swelled suddenly and he felt a strange beating in his heart.

This girl, this stranger! She was helpless, dependent on him and his strength. He would guard her and protect her with his life. His arms were around her and no one should take her from him—no one! Not the Tsar himself! She was breathing, she was there; she was a woman and he was a man, and his strength was as the strength of a lion. What harm could befall her?

He bent his head on his breast and his lips touched her hair. Across the sodden floor of the prison, suddenly, came the first rays of dawn falling aslant, touching the shadows, the two figures crouching, the rats as they fled.

Olive M. Briggs

Velasco drew the cloak closer about the sleeping form of the girl, with a tender, protecting gesture. His eyes were alert. He had forgotten himself; he had forgotten his violin; he had forgotten his art. He was facing the sunlight grim and determined.

CHAPTER VII

The office of the Polkovnik was small and narrow, low, with ceiling and walls hewn out of the rock. At one end was a window barred, looking out upon a court; at the opposite end the door. On either side of the door stood a soldier in Cossack uniform, huge fellows, sabred, with their helmets belted under their chins, and their fierce, black eyes staring straight ahead, scarcely blinking.

In the centre of the room was a table, and before the table an officer seated, also in uniform, but his head was bare and his helmet lay on the litter of papers at his elbow. He had a long, ugly face with a swarthy complexion, and eyes that were sharp and cold like steel, piercing as the point of a rapier and cruel. He was tossing the litter of papers impatiently, examining one after another at intervals, then pushing them back. He was evidently waiting, and as he waited he swore to himself under his breath, glancing from time to time at the Cossacks; but they stood stiff and immovable like marble, looking neither to right nor to left. Presently the officer leaned forward and touched a bell on the table.

"There is no use waiting any longer," he said curtly, "Bring them in."

The hammer of the bell was still tinkling when the door

swung back suddenly on its hinges and two people, a man and a woman, were half led, half dragged into the room; the Cossacks prodding them on with the blunt edge of their sabres.

"Brr—" said the officer sharply.

In a flash the Cossacks had leaped to their niches, their forms rigid and motionless, only the tassels on their helmets quivering slightly to show that they had stirred. The man and the woman were left beside the table.

"Your names?" demanded the officer, "The woman first."

The girl drew herself up wearily; her face was wan in the morning light, and her hair fell about her shoulders, dishevelled, a bright golden mass, curling about her forehead and ears in little rings and spirals like the tendrils of a vine. Her eyes were proud and she looked the officer full in the face, her hands clenched. Her voice rang full and scornful.

"My name is the Countess Kaya and I am the daughter of General Mezkarpin. What have you to say to me?"

"We have a good deal to say to you, Madame," retorted the Cossack, "if it is true that you are the Countess. I never saw her myself, but the Chief will be here presently. He knows her very eye-lashes, and if you have lied—"

"I have not lied," cried the girl, "How dare you speak to me like that! Send for my father, do you hear me? At once! The General Mezkarpin." She repeated the name distinctly and her shoulders stiffened, her blue eyes flashed. "A friend of the Tsar as you are aware. Be careful! What you do, what you say, every act, every word shall be reported to him."

"If you have not lied," continued the Cossack smoothly, "it will be still worse for you, far worse!" He began smiling to himself and twirling his mustache. "If it is true, this report, I doubt if you leave here alive, Madame, unless it is for the Mines. You have an ugly crime at your door. How you ever escaped is a wonder! The Chief has been on your track for some time, but he was late as usual; he is always slow about arresting the women, especially if they are—"

The Cossack showed his teeth suddenly in a loud laugh, leering at the slim, young figure before him. The girl blanched to the lips.

"A crime!" she said, "What crime?"

Then she put out her hand slowly, shrinkingly, and touched the figure beside her as if to make sure that he was there.

The man was standing dazed, staring from the girl to the Cossack and back again. Mezkarpin's daughter, the great Mezkarpin, the friend of Nicholas! And accused of—what? It was a mistake—nothing! He passed his hand over his eyes.

"Is this woman your wife?" said the officer shortly, "Answer."

"She is my wife."

"Where are the papers?"

The man unbuttoned his coat and felt in his breast pocket, the left, the right; then the pockets of his vest.

"I have them here, somewhere," he stammered, "Where in the devil! They were here last night!"

Olive M. Briggs

He felt again desperately. "They seem to be gone! What can have become of them? I put them here—here!" He searched again.

"Curious!" said the official, "Ha ha!"

The prisoner stared at him for a moment blinking. "You impudent scoundrel!" he cried, "She is my wife, papers or no papers. Ask her!—Kaya!"

The girl held herself straight and aloof. She was gazing down at the litter of papers on the table; her face was white and her lips were clenched in her teeth.

"Kaya—tell him! The papers are lost! God, they are gone somehow! Tell him—"

The girl released her lip and her voice came out suddenly, ringing, clear as if the room had been large and the Cossack deaf; it seemed to burst from her throat.

"I am not his wife," she said, "He is mistaken. He is telling you that out of kindness. Monsieur is a stranger to me, until last night a perfect stranger. I don't know him at all. Don't believe what he says. You see for yourself there are no papers. Is it likely?"

The tones of her voice seemed to die away suddenly and a drop of blood oozed from her lip. She wiped it away and clinched her teeth again, fiercely, as if hedging her words.

"Kaya!" cried the man. "She is my wife, I tell you, she is my wife! The priest married us. I can prove it."

"Silence," cried the Cossack. "What do we care if you are married or not. You will be imprisoned anyway for meddling in a matter that does not concern you. Silence, I tell you. Answer my questions. What is your name?"

"My name is Velasco."

"Ha—the musician?"

"Yes."

"Very good! Try again. There is only one Velasco in Russia, as every one knows, and he isn't here. Your name? Tell the truth if you can."

"My name is Velasco."

"The devil it is!" cried the Cossack, "Ha ha!—You two make a pair between you. Velasco! The Wizard of the bow! The one all Russia is mad over! Ye saints! I would give my old cavalry boots to have heard him. Bah—you anarchist dog! Now, damn you, answer me straight or I'll make you. Your name?"

The Cossack leaned over the desk, his eyes blazing fiercely, shaking his fist. "No nonsense now; do you think we can't prove it? Quick—your name?"

The prisoner folded his arms and stared up at the cross-barred window, half closing his eyes. The brows seemed to swell, to weigh down the lids.

"Will you answer or not?"

Velasco swayed a little and a dark gleam shot out between the slits: "If I had been brought up a soldier," he said, "instead of a musician, I should take pleasure in knocking you down; as it is, my muscles were trained to much better

Olive M. Briggs

purpose. This interview, sir, is becoming unpleasant. I will trouble you to send for my Stradivarius at once. Some of your men stole it, I fancy, last night. It is worth its weight twice over in gold. There is not another like it in the country, perhaps in the world. The next time his majesty, the Tsar, requests my presence, I shall inform him that the violin is here in his fortress, stolen by a slovenly, insolent official, who doesn't know a violin from a block of wood, or a note from a pin head." His eyes drooped again. The Cossack examined him narrowly.

"If you are Velasco," he said after a little, "Khorosho[1]! then prove it. There was a case brought in last night, it might have been a fiddle. Brr—Ivanovitch, go for it. No. 17,369, in the third compartment, by the wall. That isn't a bad idea!" He rubbed his hands together and laughed, showing his teeth like a wolf: "There is only the one Velasco and I know a thing or two about music in spite of your impudence. You can't cheat me." He laughed loud and long.

Velasco stood imperturbable, his arms folded; he seemed to be dreaming, his mind far away. The words fell on his ear like drops of water on a roof, rolling off, leaving no sign.

The girl looked up at him and her lips quivered slightly. She pressed them with her handkerchief and again a drop of blood blotted the white; then she drew them in with her teeth and drooped her head wearily, the confusion of her hair encircling it like a framing of gold, veiling her brow and her cheeks.

"Ah, here is Ivanovitch," cried the Cossack, "and here is the fiddle. Now, for a lark! Brr—Milikai, go for the Colonel, he is musical—ha ha! No, stop! I will keep the fun to myself. Shut the door. Is the Chief here yet?"

"No, Gospodin."

"Sapristi! Never mind, shut the door—shut the door!"

Velasco roused suddenly. He looked about him, dazed for a moment; then he sprang forward, attacking the Cossack and tearing the case from his hands. His eyes were bright and eager; his voice coming in little leaps from his throat, full of joy and relief.

"My violin, my treasure! My beloved, give it to me! You brute, you great hulking savage, if it is damaged or broken, I'll kill you! Out of my way! Let it go—or I'll strike you!— Let go!"

He snatched the case to his breast and carried it over to the table, opening it, unfolding the wrappings. They were silken and heavy. The violin lay swathed in them, the glossy arch of its body glistening yellow, golden and resinous. He touched it tenderly, lifting it, examining it, absorbed, engrossed, like a mother a child that has been bruised.

The official stared at him in amazement; the Cossacks gaped under their helmets. The girl watched him with wistful eyes. She understood. It was the artist-temperament in full command. The man had vanished, the musician was in possession. He was rocked by it, swayed, overpowered, a slave. His eyes saw nothing; his ears heard nothing; his mind was a whirl, a wonderful chaos of sound, of colour, of notes dancing, leaping.

The bow was in his hand, the violin was on his breast. He closed his eyes, swaying, pressing it to his cheek. The eyes of the girl filled with tears. It was just as he had said. He was talking to it and it was answering him, softly at first, faint and low, his fingers scarcely touching the strings; then the

Olive M. Briggs

tones burst out, full, radiant, like a bud into bloom, rushing, soaring, echoing up to the walls of the room, striking the stone, bounding back, dying away. He was drunk, he was mad; he was clasping the thing, forcing it, pressing it, swaying it, and the strings leaped after his will.

She fell back against the wall, steadying herself, and her eyes drank in the sight of him as her ears the sound—the slight, swaying figure, the dark head bowed with his hair like a mane, the arm with the bow, the abandon of the wrist, the white, flashing fingers. She drew a quick breath.

The official sat open-mouthed. The cruelty had gone from his face, the sharp, steely look from his eyes. He was grasping the desk with both hands, leaning forward, staring as one who is benumbed, hypnotized.

Velasco played as he had never played before. He was playing for his life, his identity, his freedom; and suddenly into the tones crept another consciousness, subtle at first, scarcely heard, something fragile and weak, new born as if struggling for breath. He stopped and passed his hand over his eyes, dropping the bow. Where was he! What had happened! Was it his life, or hers, he was playing to save?— Oh God!

He gazed at her across the room, into the two deep wells of her eyes, and again his muscles swelled, his chin stiffened. He stood there gazing, struggling with himself; his one personality against the other; the hair falling over his brows, the violin clasped in his arms.

Suddenly there came a knock at the door.

The Cossack gave a long sigh. He went up to Velasco slowly and took his hand, the hand with the bow.

"Great heaven!" he cried, "I am exhausted, I am limp as a rag! There is not another soul in Russia, in the world, who can play like that! You are marvellous, wonderful! All they said was too little. Monsieur—there is no further doubt in my mind, I ask your forgiveness. You are, you can be no other than he—Velasco."

The knock was repeated.

"Come in!" cried the Cossack. His voice was hoarse and he cleared his throat: "Come in!"

The door opened and General Mezkarpin strode into the room, followed by the Chief of the Third Section. The Cossacks saluted with their hands stiffly laid to their helmets; the officer stepped forward to meet them, bowing. All the assurance was gone from his manner; he was now the servant, the soldier in the presence of his superior. The General waved him aside. His face was florid and red; he was a large man, heavy, with prominent features, and his sword clanked against the stone of the floor as he moved. The girl was still leaning against the wall.

When she saw him she gave a little cry and sprang forward, stretching out her hands: "Father!" she cried, "Father!" And then she stopped suddenly and clasped her hands to her breast.

"Is this the woman you meant?" said the General, turning to Boris. He spoke as if he were on the parade-ground, every word sharp, caustic, staccato.

"Right, left, shoulder arms, march!"—"Is this the woman?"

"It is, General."

Olive M. Briggs

"She was in the Duke's room?"

"She was."

"You found her in the train?"

"In the train, last night, with this man."

"You say she is an anarchist?"

"We have known it for some time, sir."

The face of the General turned purple suddenly and the rims of his eyes were red like blood. He approached the girl and stood over her, his fists clenched, as if he would have struck her, controlling himself with a difficult effort.

"You heard?" he said, still more sharply, every word rolling out apart, detached. "Is it true? Are you mixed up with this infernal Revolutionary business? My daughter! An anarchist against the Tsar? Look me in the eyes and answer. May all the curses of heaven strike you if it is true."

The girl looked him in the eyes, her blue ones veiled and dark, gazing straight into the blood-rimmed ones above her. "It is true," she said, "I am an anarchist."

The purple tint spread over the face of the General, turning crimson in blotches. His limbs seemed to tremble under his weight; his fist came nearer.

"You fired the shot?" he cried, "You! Answer me, on your soul—the truth. It was you who murdered the Grand-Duke Stepan? You?"

The girl's face grew slowly whiter and whiter; the gold of her hair fell about her, her lips were parted and quivering. Still she looked at him and signed an assent.

"You—you shot the Grand-Duke?"

Her lips moved and she bowed her head.

The General stood paralyzed with horror. He was like one on the verge of apoplexy; his tongue stammered, his limbs refused to move. Then he drew back slowly, inch by inch, and stared at the girl with the anger and passion growing in his eyes.

"You are no daughter of mine!" he cried stammering, "You are a murderess, a criminal! You have killed the Grand-Duke—in his own house you have killed him!"

"Father!—Father!"

He gasped and put his hand to his throat. "Be still! I am not your father. You are no child of mine. I curse you—with my last breath I curse you.—Do with her as you like."

He turned to the Chief, staggering like a drunken man, panting. "Take her away—Take her out of my sight. Send her to Siberia, to the Mines—anywhere! Let her pay the uttermost penalty! Let her die! She is nothing to me!—Curse her!—Curse her!—Curse her!"

The Chief made a sign to the Cossacks and they sprang forward, one on either side of the girl. She shrank back.

"Father!" she cried.

"Chort vozmi, I am not your father! Take her away, I tell you." With a stifled oath the General flung his hands to his head and rushed from the room.

Velasco still stood dazed, clasping his violin. He was shivering as though he had a chill, and the roughness, the brutality of the words, the slamming of the door, went through him like a knife. He dropped his violin on the litter of papers.

"By heaven!" he cried, "What a terrible thing! What brutes you all are! She is my wife—mine! No matter what she has done, she is my wife. Let go of her you savages!—Kaya! Help her, some of you—don't let them take her! They are dragging her away!—Kaya! Stop them—stop them!"

He was struggling like a madman in the arms of the official, fighting with all his strength; but the muscles of the Cossack were like iron, they held him in a vice. The Chief sprang forward. They held him, and the girl was dragged from the room, brutally, roughly with blows.

She looked back over her shoulder and her eyes, with a strange, tense look, gazed deep into Velasco's. They were dark and blue, full of anguish. Her whole soul was in them; they were beseeching him, they were thanking him, they were saying goodbye. He struggled towards her. A moment—and she was gone.

The great door swung back on its hinges, the latch clicked.

A faint, low cry came back from the distance.

Velasco's arms dropped to his side and he stared fiercely from one official to the other. He tried to speak and could not. The cry came back to him, and as he heard it, his throat throbbed, his heart seemed to stop beating.

"You can go now," said the official. "We know who you are, and there is nothing against you."

He whispered something to the Chief. They handed him his violin and his case with its wrappings, and led him to the door. He followed them out, up the winding steps, through the passages, out into the court, stumbling blindly.

"You can go—there is nothing against you."

He walked straight on with his head bent forward, his eyes on the ground. He clasped the violin in one hand, the case with the other. He was shivering.

The cry followed him out into the street. It rang in his ears. Her eyes were gazing into his with a strange tenseness. He could feel them. He was dumb, he was helpless.

Oh God—the cry again! It was low, it was faint, it was broken with pain. He stumbled on.

[1] Very well.

Olive M. Briggs

CHAPTER VIII

"Is Monsieur Velasco in?"

"He is, sir."

"Tell him his manager, Galitsin, is here and must speak to him at once."

"Very well, Barin, but—he is composing. He has been composing for days—Monsieur knows?"

"I know," said the Manager.

He was a short, thick-set man with crisp, curly hair, a wide mouth, a blunt nose, and eyes that twinkled perpetually as though at some inward joke that he did not share with the rest of the world; they twinkled now and he snapped his fingers.

"Go ahead, Bobo, you coward. If he insists on hurling a boot at your head, why dodge it—dodge it! Or wait, stay where you are. I will announce myself."

The old servant retreated with alacrity down the hallway, stepping lightly as if on eggs with his finger on his lips, while the Manager opened the Studio door softly, without knocking, and closed it behind him.

Before the fire-place, with his back to the door, sat Velasco. His shoulders were bent, his head was in his hands; he was motionless. The Manager cleared his throat slowly with emphasis:

"Eh, Velasco, is that you?"

The young Musician leaped to his feet as if struck by a blow, and faced the intruder angrily, tossing the hair away from his brows. His face was pale, as of one who has watched instead of sleeping, and his eyes were haggard and bloodshot.

"A hundred devils take you!" he cried, "What are you doing here? I told Bobo to keep people out, the treacherous rascal! For heavens sake go and leave me in peace; I tell you Galitsin, go! Don't come near me."

The Manager laughed: "Composing, Velasco?"

"Can't you see it? Of course I am composing. Go!" He waved his hand towards the door. "Don't talk."

"You must talk with me," exclaimed the Manager briskly, "Now Velasco, there's no use, you will have to listen to reason. The way you are behaving is outrageous, abominable! All your German engagements have gone to the wall. My desk is piled high with letters; the agents are furious. In Leipzig the Gewandhaus was entirely sold out a fortnight ago. In Dresden there isn't a seat left. Why the money loss is something tremendous! I had a telegram this morning; they are nearly crazy. You must keep your engagements; you will ruin your career utterly, absolutely. You will never dare show your face in Germany again. And here you sit composing—composing! Good heavens, you look like it!

　　　　　Olive M. Briggs

You look as if you had been on a bat for a week! You look drunk, Velasco, drunk! I never saw such a change in a man! Come—wake up! Rouse yourself! Take the train tonight."

The Manager laid his arm on the young Musician's shoulder and patted it soothingly.

"Take the night train, Velasco. You ought to be playing, not composing! You know that as well as I do. If you go tonight, you will reach Leipzig in time. It makes a difference of thousands of roubles to me as well as to you; remember that. You musicians have no conscience. Come, Velasco—are you listening?"

The Musician stood listless, his hands in his pockets, staring down at the bricks of the chimney piece.

"What is that?" he exclaimed, "Were you speaking?—Oh, damn you, Galitsin, why don't you go? I'm not a slave! I won't stir one step in Germany if I don't feel like it; I swear I won't! Cancel everything, everything. Heavens! I couldn't play if I tried! You managers are like the old man of the mountain; you want to sit on my neck and lash me on as if I were Sinbad. All for the sake of a few dirty roubles to put in your pocket! What do I care? I won't do it, I tell you. Go and manage somebody else; get another slave. Petrokoff over there in Moscow! He will be like a little lamb and eat out of your hand. Now be off—be off! Your voice is like a bee buzzing."

Velasco threw himself back in his chair again and blinked defiantly up at the Manager through his bloodshot eyes. They were heavy and weary, he could scarcely keep them open; his fingers strummed against the arm of the chair and he began to whistle to himself softly, a quaint little Polish air like a folk-song. Galitsin shook his head frowning:

"You are a perfect child, Velasco, when this mood gets hold of you. There is no doing anything with you. Very well then, I wash my hands of the whole business. Answer your own letters and satisfy the agents, if you can. Tell them you are ill, dying, dead—anything you please."

"Bah!" said Velasco, "Don't answer them at all." He shut his eyes.

The Manager gave a hasty glance about the Studio and then he bent his head to the chair, whispering:

"You have acted badly enough before, heaven knows, but never like this. It is not the composing. Where is the score?—Not a note!" He breathed a few words in Velasco's ear and the Musician started up.

"How did you know; who told you? The devil take you, Galitsin!"

The Manager smiled, running his hands through his short, crisp curls. "Everyone knows; all St. Petersburg is talking about it. When a man of your fame, Velasco, insists on befriending a Countess, and one who is the daughter of Mezkarpin, and an anarchist to boot—"

He spread out his hands: "Ah, she is beautiful, I know. I saw her at the Mariinski. She stared at you as if she were bewitched. You had every excuse; but get down on your knees, Velasco, and give thanks. It is no fault of yours that you are not tramping through the snow to Siberia now, just as she is. A lesser man, one whose career was less marked! By heaven, Velasco, what is it?—You are choking me!"

"Say it again!" cried the Musician, "You know where she is? Tell me! By God, will you tell me, or not?—I'll force it out

Olive M. Briggs

of you!"

"Let go of my throat!" gasped the Manager. "Sit down, Velasco! Don't be so excitable, so violent! No wonder you play with such passion; but I am not a violin, if you please. Take your hands off my throat and sit down."

"Where is she?"

Galitsin straightened his collar and necktie before the mirror of the mantel-piece. "What is the matter with you, Velasco? Any one would suppose you were in love with her! Better not; she is doomed—she is practically dead."

"Dead!"

"Don't fly up like that!—Sit down! I saw the Chief of Police yesterday, and he gave me some advice to hand on to you."

"Is she dead, Galitsin?"

"No, but she will be. She is sent with a gang to the Ekaterinski Zavad. They are gone already, chained together, and marching through the snow and the cold. It is thousands of miles. A Countess, who has undoubtedly never taken a step in her life without a maid—who knows! She is frail, she won't live to get there."

The room was still for a moment and suddenly a coal fell from the fire to the hearth with a thud, flaring up. Then it broke into ashes. Presently the Manager continued:

"She shot the Grand-Duke Stepan, they say. I don't know. The thing has been hushed up for the sake of Mezkarpin, poor man! The Chief told me he had had a stroke in the prison and may not recover. The girl must be a tigress!—

Velasco! Are you asleep?—Wake up!—Velasco!"

"What mines did you say, Galitsin?"

"The Ekaterinski Zavad."

"They have started already?"

"Yesterday."

"The Chief told you that?"

"The Chief himself told me."

"Did he mention the route?"

"By the old road through Tobolsk, I dare say, the usual one.
Come, Velasco, don't brood over it!"

"Were they chained?"

The Musician shuddered and moved his limbs uneasily.
"Chains, Galitsin? Fancy, how horrible! How they must
clank! It must be maddening—jingling, rattling with every
step—Ah!"

The Manager shrugged his shoulders. "When a woman
undertakes to murder the Grand-Duke Stepan, what else can
she expect? Mezkarpin is a friend of the Tsar, otherwise she
would have been hung, or shot!—Why of course! The Chief
said she was utterly brazen about it. She asked over and over
if he were dead, and then said she was glad. Lucky for you,
Velasco, they recognized you, they didn't take you for an
accomplice; you would never have touched a violin again.
All the same—"

Olive M. Briggs

He glanced around the Studio again and his voice grew lower: "The Chief gave warning. You are to leave Russia, he said. Velasco—listen to me! He said you must leave Russia at once, to-night—do you hear?"

The Manager leaned forward and shook the Musician's shoulder angrily. "Velasco, do you hear?—If you won't go for your Art, you must go for your safety.—Do you hear me? You must!"

"I hear you," said Velasco, "You needn't bellow in my ear like a bull! If I must, I suppose I must. Go and write your letters and leave me in peace."

"Shall I tell the agents you are coming?"

"Tell them anything you like. Pull me about on wires like a little tin puppet, and set me down anywhere in Europe, just as you please. I feel like an automaton! You will be winding up my Stradivarius next with a key. Now go, or I won't stir a step!"

The Manager took up his gloves and cane; he seemed uneasy. "You swear you will start to-night, Velasco?"

"Be off!"

"By the night train? I shall meet you at the station."

"Very well. Good-bye."

"The Night Express?"

The Musician closed his eyes and nodded. "You cackle like an old woman, Galitsin; you would talk a cricket dumb. Send me up Bobo, if you see him, will you?—Good-bye."

Galitsin took out his watch. "In three hours then," he said, "Au revoir! You have plenty of time to pack. Eleven thirty, Velasco."

The door closed behind the short, thick-set figure with the crisp, curling hair, and the Musician waited in his chair. Presently the door opened again.

"Is that you, Bobo,—eh? Come in. I sent for you. Didn't you tell me your wife was ill?"

"Yes, Barin."

"You would like to go to her to-night?—Well, go. I shan't need you. Don't jabber, you make my head spin. Go at once and stay until morning; leave the cigarettes on the tray and the wine on the table—that is all. Just take yourself off and quietly."

After a moment or two the door closed, and the sound of footsteps, scuffling in list slippers, died slowly away in the corridor. Velasco leaned forward with his head in his hands, his bloodshot eyes staring into the coals.

"He may be one of them," he murmured, "or he may not. You can't trust people. He is better out of the way."

The haggard look had deepened on his face; then he rose suddenly from his chair and went into the next room, dropping the curtain behind him. There were sounds in the room as of the pulling out of drawers, the creaking of keys in a rusty lock, steps hurrying from one spot to another, the fall of a heavy boot. Then presently the curtain was drawn aside and he reappeared.

No, it was not Velasco; it was some one else, a gypsey in a

rakish costume. The mane of black hair was clipped close to his head; he wore a scarf about his waist, a shabby jacket of velveteen on his back; his trousers were short to the knees, old and spotted; his boots were worn at the heel and patched. It wasn't Velasco—it was a gypsey, a tattered, beggarly ragamuffin, with dark, brooding eyes and a laugh on his lips, a laugh that was like a twist of the muscles.

He crossed the room stealthily on his tiptoes, glancing about him, and stood before the mirror examining himself. At the first glance he laughed out loud; then he clapped his hand over his mouth, listening again. But he was alone, and the form reflected in the mirror was his own, no shadow behind. He snatched up the lamp and held it close to the glass, peering at himself from the crown of his close-cropped head to the patch on his boot. He gazed at the scarf admiringly; it was red with tassels, and he patted it with his free hand.

"That is how they do it!" he cried softly, laughing. "It is perfect. I don't know myself! Ha ha!—I would cheat my own shadow. If the door should open now, and Galitsin should come in—the ox! How he would stare! And Bobo, poor devil, he would take me for a thief in my own Studio.—God, what is that?—a step on the stairs! The police! They come preying like beasts and seize one at night. She told me!"

The gypsey's hand trembled and shook, and the wick of the lamp flared up. Great heaven! The step crept nearer—it was at the door—the door moved! It was opening!

He dropped the lamp with a crash; the light went out and he staggered back against the wall, clutching his scarf, straining his ears to hear in the darkness.

The door opened wider.

Some one slipped through it and closed it again, and the step came nearer, creaking on the boards. He heard the soft patter of hands feeling their way, the faint sound of a breath. It was worse than in the carriage, because the room was so large and the matches were on the table, far off. There was no way of seeing, or feeling. The step came nearer.

If it was a spy, he could grapple with him and throw him. The gypsey took a step forward towards the other step, and all of a sudden two bodies came together, grappling, wrestling. Two cries went up, the one loud, the other faint like an echo.

"Hush, it is I, Velasco! You are soft like a woman! Your hair—It is you, Kaya! It is you! I know your voice—your touch! Did you hear the lamp crash? Wait! Let me light a candle."

He stumbled over to the table, feeling his way, clutching the soft thing by the arm, the shoulder.

"It is you, Kaya, tell me, it is you! Damn the match, it is damp, how it sputters!—Put your face close, let me see it. Kaya! Is it you, yourself?"

The two faces stared at one another in the flickering light, almost touching; then the other sprang back with a cry of dismay.

"You are a gypsey, you are not Velasco! The voice is his,— Dieu! And the eyes—they are his, and the brows! Let me go! Don't laugh—let me go!"

"No—no, Kaya, come back! It is I. They told me you were chained with a gang; and were walking through the snow and the cold to the mines. How did you escape; how could you escape?"

"Yes—it is you," said the girl, "I see now. It was the costume, and your hair is all cut. I thought you had gone in the train to Germany." She shuddered and clung to his hand. "Why do you wear that? Why aren't you gone? The Studio was vacant, I thought—deserted, or I shouldn't have come!"

Velasco gazed at her, chafing the cold, soft fingers between his own. "Oh God, how I have suffered! I tried to reach you, I did everything, and then I shut myself up here waiting—I was nearly mad. Kaya—you escaped from the fortress alone, by yourself? Did they hurt you? You cried out; it rings in my ears—that cry! It has never left me! I shut myself up and paced the floor. Did they hurt you?"

The girl looked over her shoulder: "It was horrible, alone," she breathed, "Some of the guards, the sentinels, belong to us. Hush—no one knows; it must never be guessed. To-night, after dark, someone whistled—one was waiting for me in the corridor with the keys; the others were drugged. They handed me on to someone outside; I was dropped like a pebble over the wall. Then I ran—straight here I ran."

She put her hand to her breast. "Why aren't you gone? Go now, to-night. Leave me here. As soon as it is light I shall be missed, and then—" She shuddered and her hand trembled in his, like a bird that is caught, soft and quivering.

Velasco looked at her again and then he looked away at the candle: "I won't leave you," he said, "and the railroad is useless. They would track us at once. When I put this on—" He began smoothing the scarf. "I meant to follow you through the snow and the cold to the mines, like a beggar musician."

He laughed: "You didn't know me yourself, you see? I was safe."

"Monsieur Velasco, you were coming to me? Ah, but they told you a lie! I—" She breathed a few words to him softly.

"They would have—"

She nodded.

"When?"

"To-morrow at daybreak."

"In spite of Mezkarpin?"

She broke down and buried her face in her hands.

Velasco began to pace the room slowly. "If you had a costume like mine," he said, "If your hair were cut—" Then he brightened suddenly and ran forward to the girl, snatching her hands from her eyes, dragging her to her feet.

"What a fool I was!" he cried, "What an idiot! Quick, Kaya! My chum is an artist; he is off now in Sicily, painting the rocks, and the sea, and the peasants; but his things are all there in his room next to mine, just duds for his models you know. Go—go! Put on one like mine. You shall be a boy. We will be boys together, gypsies, and play for our living. We will walk to the frontier, Kaya, together."

The two stared at one another for a moment. He was pushing her gently towards the curtain. "Quick!" he whispered, "Be quick!" They both listened for a moment.

Then he pushed her inside and dragged down the curtain:

Olive M. Briggs

"Now, I must pack," he cried, "Now I must prepare to meet Galitsin, the round-eyed ox! Ha ha!—He will wait until he is stiff, and then he will fly back here in a rage. Good God, we must hurry!" He began opening and shutting the drawers, taking out money and jewels from one, articles of apparel from another.

"No collars, no neck-ties!" he said to himself, "How simple to be a gypsey! A knapsack will hold all for her and for me.—Kaya!—Bozhe moi!"

The curtain was drawn back and in the doorway stood a boy.

CHAPTER IX

The two gypsies gazed at one another in silence.

The small, picturesque figure in the doorway wore velveteen trousers of green, old and faded, a black jacket rusty, with the sleeves patched, and a scarlet sash tied loosely about the waist. On the back of her cropped yellow curls was a velveteen cap, rakishly tipped, and she stood debonair beneath the folds of the curtain with a laugh on her lips.

"Mon Dieu!" she cried, "How you stare, Monsieur! Will I do? What sort of a boy do I make; all right? Are you satisfied, sir?"

She made a little rush forward, eluding Velasco, and stopped before the mirror with her hands boyishly deep in her pockets, glancing back over her shoulder and pirouetting slowly backwards and forwards.

"The hair looks a little rough!" she exclaimed, "I cut it with a pair of shears, or perhaps it was a razor, who knows! Ma foi! It is not like a girl's at all, so short! What my maid would say! You would never take me for a Countess now, would you—would you?" She patted her curls and pulled down her jacket in front, turning first to one side, then to the other. "What a nice pair of gypsies we make, sir, eh? Come and

Olive M. Briggs

look at yourself. You are taller than I, and bigger, and you have such shoulders, heavens! Mine are not half the size. You mustn't bully me, you know, not if I am a boy. You took the best jacket, the biggest, and look what I have—such a little one, only patches and rags! And see what boots!"

She held out one slim, small foot in a peasant's boot and inspected it, pointing to the sole with little exclamations of horror. "I took the only ones I could find, and see—" Then she looked at him coaxingly with her eyes half veiled by her lashes, sideways, as if afraid of his gaze.

"Do I make a nice boy, Monsieur, tell me? Am I just like a gypsy, the real ones? Is it right, do you think?" She faltered.

Velasco took a step forward and looked down at the reflection in the mirror, the profile averted, the flush on her cheek, the curls on her brow, the boyish swagger and the hands in the pockets, the cap on the back of the tilted head, the laughing eyes, half veiled. He towered above her, gazing. And presently her eyes crept up to his under the lashes and they met in the mirror. She drew slowly away.

"How little you are!" he cried, "You never seemed so little before; in a cloak, in a veil, you were tall. And now, stand still, let me measure. Your cap just reaches my shoulder. Kaya—"

She gave a gay little laugh and held her back against his. "How you cheat!" she cried, "No—your heels on the floor, sir—there, now! Back to back, can you see in the mirror? Where do I come?"

The two stood motionless for a moment, their shoulders touching, peering eagerly sideways into the glass.

"Kaya, you are standing on tiptoe!"

"No—it is you."

"Kaya! You rogue!"

She gave a little cry, laughing out like a child caught in mischief, springing away. "I must practise being a boy," she exclaimed, "What is it you do? It is so different from being a Countess. One feels so free. No heels, no train, no veil! When one is used to the boots it must be heaven. If my cap would only stay on!"

She began to roam over the room, taking boyish strides, puckering her lips in a whistle; her thumbs in her vest and her head thrown back. "There, now, that is it; I feel better already, quite like a man. It is charming, Monsieur; a little more practice—"

Velasco was following her about with the cap in his hands. "Step softly, Kaya, step softly," he said, "Stand still. Let me put it on for you."

"No—no, toss it over."

With a little spring the girl swung herself on the table edge, balancing and swinging her feet; looking up at him from under her lashes and laughing.

"Shall I make a good comrade, Monsieur Velasco? What do you think?"

He leaned over the table towards her. His eyes were bright and eager, searching her face, the dimples that came and went in her cheeks, her soft, white throat, bare under the collarless jacket; the lips parted, and red, and arched; the rings of her hair, shining like gold.

"Kaya," he whispered hoarsely, "I never saw you like this before. My little comrade, my friend, my—We will tramp together, you and I—all the way to the frontier. They will never suspect us, never! The Stradivarius shall earn our bread, and if you are ill, or weary, I will carry you in my arms. In the market-places I will play for the peasants to dance, and you—you, Kaya—ah, what will you do?"

He laughed softly to himself and began teasing her, half gayly, half tenderly, with his face close to hers, the sleeve of his jacket brushing her arm.

"What will you do, Kaya? Look at me! Your cheek is red like a rose; your eyes are like stars. Don't turn them away. Lift the fringe of those lashes and look at me, Kaya. Will you pass the cap for the pennies?—You will have to doff it because you are a boy; and you must do something because you are a gypsey. Will you pass the cap for the peasants to pay?"

He held the velveteen cap in his hands, playing with it, caressing it, watching her. "Look at me, Kaya!"

She flushed and drew back, her heart beating in little throbs under the vest. Suddenly she turned and looked at him squarely. It was strange, whenever their eyes met, like a thrill, a shock, an ecstasy; and then a slow returning to consciousness as after a blow.

All at once, she drooped her lashes and began to trill, softly, faintly, like a bird, the tones clear, and sweet, and high; and as she sang, she glanced at him under her lashes, with her head on one side. The voice pulsed and grew in her throat, swelling out; then she softened it quickly with a look over her shoulder, half fearfully, and again it soared to a high note, trilling, lingering and dropping at last.

Her mouth scarcely opened. The sound seemed to come through the arch of her lips, every note pure, and sweet, and soft like a breath. Velasco bent over entranced.

"How you sing!" he cried, "Like some beautiful bird! In Italy, on the shores of the lakes, I have heard the nightingales sing like that; but never a woman. The timbre is crystal and pure, like clear, running water. When you soar to the heights, it is like a lark flying; and when you drop into alt, it is a tone that forces the tears to one's eyes, so pathetic and strange. Who taught you, Kaya? Who taught you to sing like that? Or were you born so with a voice alive in your throat; you had only to open it and let it come out?"

She shook her head, swinging her feet, trying to laugh.

"It is so small," she said wistfully. "You are a musician, Monsieur Velasco, and I—I know nothing of music. No—I will pass the cap for pennies. Give it to me. Is it getting late, must we go?"

She took the cap and put it on her head, on the back of her curls, avoiding his eyes. "Will that do for a gypsey? Is it straight—Velasco?" She said the name quite low and breathed hurriedly, with a flush on her cheeks.

He was still staring at her, but he said nothing; he made no motion and she drew away from him a little frightened.

"You are like a violin," he murmured, "I told you you were like a violin. You are all music, as I am music. We will make music together—Kaya. Sing for me again, just open your lips and breathe—once more! Let me hear you trill?"

Olive M. Briggs

"I can't," said the girl. "I am faint, Velasco. When I look at you now there is a mist before my eyes. The room sways." She put out her hands suddenly, as if to steady herself.

Velasco started back: "Good heavens, Kaya, what is the matter? The colour has gone from your cheeks; there are shadows under your eyes, deep and heavy as though they were painted. Don't faint, will you? Don't! I shouldn't know what under heaven to do!"

The girl slipped down from the table and, staggering a little, threw herself into the chair by the fire-place. "Get me some food, Velasco; some bread, some wine. In a moment it will pass!" She began laughing again immediately. "Don't be frightened. It is you who are pale, not I. Just a morsel to eat—Velasco. Since last night I have eaten nothing. You forget how hungry a boy can be! Is there time?"

Velasco had snatched the red wine from the table and was pouring it out in a glass, holding it to her lips.

"Drink, Kaya, drink—and here are biscuits, shall I break them for you? Don't speak. Shut your eyes, and drink, and eat. I will feed you."

He hovered over her with little exclamations of pity and self-reproach.

"Why didn't I see at once you were starving! Poor child, poor little one! You seemed so gay, dancing about; your cheeks were so red and now—Ah no, it is better—the colour is coming back slowly. The wine brings a flush."

The girl lay back with her eyes closed, sipping the wine from the glass as he held it. "Is there plenty of time, Velasco?" she said faintly.

He looked at the hands of the malachite clock on the mantel. They pointed to ten and presently it began to strike.

"Yes—yes." he whispered, "Lie still. Let me feed you. We will go presently."

"What was that on the stairway?" she said, "Was it a noise?—I thought I heard something."

She opened her eyes and started up; and with the sudden movement, the glass in her hand tipped and spilled over. "It is nothing," she said, "It fell on my hand. I will wipe it away."

Velasco laughed. "Your hand!" he cried, "Your hand is a rose leaf, so soft and so white. The wine has stained it with a blotch. How strange! It is red, it is crimson—a spot like blood."

The girl blanched suddenly and fell back with a cry.

"Not blood, Velasco! Wipe it off! Take it away! Not blood! Oh, take it away!"

Her eyes stared down at the blotch on her hand. They were frightened, dilated, and her whole body quivered in the chair. "Velasco—take it away!"

He put down the glass and took the small, white hand in his own, brushing it gently with the sleeve of his jacket. "There now," he said, "it is gone. It was only a drop of wine. Hush—hush! See, there is no blood, Kaya, I never meant there was blood. Don't scream again!"

"It's the Cross!" she cried, "the curse of the Black Cross! Ah, go—leave me! I am a murderess! I shot him, Velasco, I shot him! I fulfilled the vow, the oath of the order. But now—oh God! I am cursed! Not blood—not blood!"

She was struggling to her feet.

"*Without weakness, without hesitation, or mercy*. I did it! Velasco—I did it!"

She fell back into the chair again, sobbing, murmuring to herself. "Not blood—no—not blood!"

"That is over and past," said Velasco, "Don't think of it, Kaya. Be a boy, a man, not weak like a woman. Eat the rest of the bread."

The girl took the bread from his hand.

"Finish the wine."

He held the glass to her lips until she had drained it; and then she began to laugh a little unsteadily.

"You are right," she said, "a boy doesn't—weep. I must be strong, a good comrade." She dashed the tears from her eyes and looked up at him pathetically, smiling with lips that still quivered. "It is over," she said, "I am—I have—you know; but it is over! I will forget it. Sometimes I can forget it if I try; then I shut my eyes at night and I see him before me, on his face with his arms outstretched—still and strange. The blood is trickling a stream on the floor! I hear the shot—I—"

"Be still, Kaya, hush! Don't speak of it; forget it! Hush!"

She began to laugh again: "See, I am your comrade, light-hearted and gay as a gypsey should be. Already—I have forgotten! What a couple of tramps we are, you and I! Just look at your boots!"

"And your faded old jacket!"

"And your scarf, Velasco!"

"And your velveteen cap!"

They laughed out together, and then they stopped suddenly and listened. "Was it anything?"

"No, I think not."

"Are you sure?"

Velasco leaned towards her and their fingers touched for a moment. She drew them away.

"Shall we go; is it time?"

"Not yet," said Velasco, "not yet! Your lips are so sweet, they are arched like a bow; they quiver like a string when one plays on it. Kiss me, Kaya."

She pressed him back with her hands outstretched, her palms against his coat. "We must go," she whispered, "They will track us, Monsieur. I am frightened."

"Kaya, kiss me."

Their eyes met and drew closer, gazing intently, the dark and the blue.

"Don't touch me," she said faintly. "We are two boys together. You must forget that I am a girl. Can you forget?"

"No," said Velasco. "You were charming before, but you are irresistible now, in that velveteen jacket and scarf, with the curls on your brow. When you look at me so, with your head on one side, and your eyes half veiled, and the flush on your cheeks, you are sweet—I love you! Kiss me."

He pressed forward closely, his eyes still on hers; but she held him back with her hands, trembling a little.

"Velasco," she whispered, "Listen! I trust you. You are stronger than I; your wrists are like steel, but—I trust you. See—I trust you."

She took down her hands from his shoulders and folded them proudly over her breast, gazing up at him.

"How strange your eyes are," said Velasco, "like two pools in the twilight; one could drown in their depths. You are there behind the blue, Kaya. Your spirit looks out at me, brave and dauntless. When you sob, you are like a child; when you look at me under the veil of your lashes and your heart beats fast, you are a woman. And now—you are—what are you, Kaya? A young knight watching beside his shield!"

He hesitated, and passed his hand over his brows, and looked at her again; then he moved away slowly and began to lay the things in his knapsack. "They are all boys' things," he said, "but you are a boy; they will do for you too."

"Yes," she said.

He laughed a little unsteadily. "There is money in my belt; now the knapsack is ready, my violin—and that is all. It is nearly eleven. Come—Kaya."

He turned his head away without looking at her; he

approached the door slowly. The girl sat still in the chair.

"Are you coming?"

There was silence; then he turned on his heel, and went back to her, and laid his hand on her shoulder. "Kaya," he said, whispering as if someone could hear, "Are you afraid? Why are you afraid to come with me, dear brother musician, dear comrade?" His voice broke. "I will take care of you. You said you would trust me, Kaya."

The girl clasped his arm with a cry: "I am not afraid for myself," she said, "but for you—you, Velasco. Leave me before it is too late. There is time for the train, just time. I implore you to go!"

She trembled and raised her eyes to his. "If anything should happen, and you suffered for me, I couldn't bear it. Leave me—Velasco!"

He put out his hand and took hers, crushing it in his own strength. He did not speak but he drew her forward, and she followed him dumbly, quietly, without resistance; her head drooping, the cap on the back of her yellow curls; the lashes hiding her eyes, fringing her cheek.

He took the Stradivarius under his arm. The door closed and they started out, hesitating, looking back over their shoulders; stealing down the stairs like two frightened children hand in hand.

Olive M. Briggs

CHAPTER X

The first pale streaks of dawn were creeping slowly up from the horizon, piercing the darkness of night with faint, far-away shafts of light, like arrows silver-tipped, shot from an unseen quiver. In the distance, the snow fields stretched limitless and vast, and between them the road wound in and out, narrow and dark, like a coiled serpent amid the whiteness.

Here and there an occasional black-roofed farm house reared its head; across the snow came the sudden gleam of an ice covered pond; while afar off, to the left, the domes of Belaia rose dark and mysterious in their roundness, like a patch of giant toadstools, shadowy and strange. The air was damp and a cold wind blew over the snow drifts. Along the road, in the full teeth of the blast, trudged two boys, the one a little behind the other, and the taller of the two shielding the younger with his body.

"Is it far now, Velasco?"

"Not far, if you peep through the folds of your cloak you will see the domes over yonder. Are you weary, Kaya?"

"No—Velasco."

The voice came in little gasps, as if blown by the gale, fluttering like a leaf that is tossed hither and thither. The older boy bent his head, struggling forward.

"The wind is like a dagger," he stammered, "it cuts through the cloak like an edge of fine steel, like a poignard piercing the heart. Come closer, Kaya, and let me put my arm around you. Your body sways like a frail stem, a flower. You are stumbling and your breath freezes, even as it comes through your lips. Come closer, or you will fall, Kaya. Let me put my arm around you."

"It is nothing, Velasco; only the snow that whirls before my eyes and blinds them. Is that the dawn, those faint, grey streaks in the distance?"

"You are stumbling again, Kaya! It is wonderful the way you have tramped the whole night through. We are almost there."

"It is only my feet, Velasco; they are frozen a little by the snow, and numb. That is nothing for a boy. Let us run a race together. Come!"

"The wind mocks at you, little one. Run in such a blast— fight rather! Put your head down and battle with it. The demon! Keep behind me a little; use my cloak and my arm as a shield. It is not far now."

"Shall we stop at the inn, Velasco; is it safe, do you think? There is one on the market-place."

"Yes, why not?"

"I was there once before, Velasco, with my—with my maid!" The girl laughed.

"You pant, Kaya, and your breath comes in jerks. Are you frightened?"

"No, Velasco—no!"

"They will look for us in the trains and the boats, but never in the snow-fields and the market-places. Kaya, we will tramp as long as you are able to bear it, and then—"

"Then—Velasco?"

"We will take the train at some smaller station—Dvisk, Vilna—wherever we can."

"You, Velasco, but not I."

"Both of us. I will never leave you again. In my pocket are passports, blank; I bribed the official. We will fill them in together: two gypsies, one dark and one fair. Ha, Kaya— keep up—a little further! See, the domes are bigger now and nearer, and the road goes straight without winding."

"Velasco—I cannot walk! I cannot see! Everything whirls before me in a mist Go! Leave me—I am falling—"

The older gypsey gave a despairing look over the snow-fields; they were bare, and white, and glistening. The golden ball of the sun had begun to climb slowly and the shafts had grown suddenly yellow. Across the icy surface of the pond the wind whistled, lashing him in the face as with a whip. The road was narrow and deserted. They were alone, and the form of the younger boy lay against him unconscious, inert, half sunk in the snow.

Velasco bent over his companion, chafing the hands, the cheeks; they were cold like ice. He gave another despairing glance around; then he lifted the form in his stiffening arms and carried it slowly, laboriously forward, plodding each step; his head bent, his teeth grit together, fighting his way.

The shafts lengthened across the sky; the domes grew larger and began to glitter in the rays of the sunlight; by the side of the road houses appeared, straggling at first, then nearer together. Suddenly, behind them, came the tinkle of sleigh-bells, and the crunching of snow beaten in by the weight of hoofs.

"Oi—Oi!"

Velasco stepped aside with his burden and stared at the sleigh as it approached. It was a cart, roughly set on runners, drawn by a pair of long-haired ponies; while fastened behind was a mare, and two wild-eyed colts following.

The peasant in the seat was wrapped in sheep-skin and smoking a short, thick pipe held between his teeth.

"Oi—Oi! Is that a corpse you hold there, Bradjaga?" he cried. His voice was hardly distinguishable above the roaring of the gale.

"For the love of heaven," shouted Velasco, "Moujik, if you have a heart under your sheep-skin, let me lay my comrade in the cart! He is faint with the cold, benumbed. We have tramped all night in the snow. Are you bound for the market at Belaia? Hey, stop! Moujik—stop!"

"Get in," said the peasant, "The ponies rear and dance as if Satan were on their backs, and the mare is like one possessed! It is good to see the sun. Get in, Bradjaga, and if the burden in your arms is no corpse it will soon become one! The night has been hell. Bozhe moi! At the first

Olive M. Briggs

crossing to the left is a tea-house—Get along you brutes!—Pour the vodka into his throat; it will sting him to life!"

The ponies dashed forward, the mare and the foals running behind. Velasco sat huddled on the floor of the cart, his violin and the knapsack slung from his shoulders; his arms still clasping the slight, dark form, protecting it from the jolting of the runners. He was muttering to it under his breath:

"Kaya—poor little one! Your curls are damp against my cheek; your forehead is ice! Courage, little comrade. Now—your heart beats faster—your eye-lids are flickering! Another moment and you will be warm and safe. The lights of the tea-house are ahead. Moujik—faster! We will drink a glass of vodka together, all three! Faster—faster!"

As the sleigh dashed into the court-yard, the great red ball of the sun rose above the distant tree-tops; and behind the stables a cock began to crow, slowly, feebly at first, as if just awake and stretching his wings.

When Kaya came to consciousness again, she was lying on a pile of straw in a low raftered room. She had dreamt that she was chained and in prison, and that something was choking her and weighing on her breast; but when she tried to move her limbs, she found that it was the blankets, wrapping her closely; and when she opened her eyes, she saw the face of Velasco bending over her, and he was trying to force some wine through her clenched lips.

"Where am I?" said Kaya faintly, "You are choking me, Velasco!"

She struggled to a sitting posture, leaning on one elbow, and peered up into his face. "What has happened?" she said again, "Where are we? I thought we were tramping through the snow and my feet were frozen! You are pale, Velasco, and your eyes are heavy!—Have I slept?"

Velasco glanced over his shoulder, and then brought his lips close to her face and whispered: "You fainted and I carried you in my arms; the Moujik brought us here in his cart. You opened your eyes once, and then when we laid you on the straw you fell asleep. You slept so long I was frightened, Kaya—if it had not been for your jacket moving under the blankets, rising and falling softly with the beat of your heart, you might have been dead; you were so still! Poor little one, you were exhausted. Drink a little and eat!"

"What time is it, Velasco?"

"The sun was rising when we drove into the court and now, in another hour or two, it will be setting."

Kaya put her hand to her cropped yellow curls, and then she looked at him and a dimple came in her cheek:

"I forgot about being a boy," she murmured, "Is this what you call an inn, Velasco? It looks like a stable!"

"It is a stable."

Kaya looked at him again and began to laugh softly: "I forgot about being a gypsey," she said, "Your clothes are ragged and torn, Velasco; they are worse than they were that night in your Studio. And I—tell me—how do I look?"

"Like a little Bradjaga, sweet, and disreputable, and boyish!"

Kaya drew herself slowly to her knees and then to her feet, brushing the straw from her velveteen trousers and the

Olive M. Briggs

sleeves of her jacket. "They wouldn't let us in the inn because we were gypsies, was that it? They were afraid we would steal?"

The dimples came back in her face and she picked up her cap from the floor, dusting it with her elbow and cramming it down on the back of her curls. "Steal me a little bread, Velasco, I am hungry."

"Come back to your nest in the straw, Kaya; put your fingers in my pocket and steal for yourself. I bought a loaf with a couple of copecks, and some honey-cake. At sun-down, when the peasants come for their vodka, there will be a dance. They have never danced to a Stradivarius before; but they won't know the difference, Kaya, not they! We will pay for the straw with a rollicking waltz—Ha ha!"

The gypsey musician caught his comrade by the arm and pulled her down on the straw beside him.

"Which pocket, Velasco? Oh, I feel the honey-cake bulging! Give it to me."

"No—take it yourself!"

"Your pocket is so deep; it is like diving into a pool."

"Not so deep as your eyes, Kaya. You thief! Ah, take your fingers away and pay for your bread."

"Are you fooling, Velasco? You look at me so strangely! Sometimes your eyes are slits and disappear under your brows, and now—Velasco, turn your head away—I am hungry. You make my heart beat!—Velasco—give me the bread."

"Pay first and then you shall have it."

She stared at him a moment, drawing back into the straw. "I am a boy," she said softly, panting, "Remember I am a boy! Don't—tease me!"

"Just once, Kaya."

"No—Velasco."

The older gypsey glanced again about the low raftered loft. The window in the rafters was hung with cob-webs; the light came through it dimly, a shaft of sun-beams dancing on the floor; they fell on her hair beneath the cap and the curls glistened like gold. Her eyes were watching him.

"No—no—Velasco!"

He came nearer to her, and the straw crackled as he moved, stretching out his arms: "When you were weary, Kaya, I carried you. When you fell asleep I watched over you. It is not your heart that is beating so fast; it is mine! The colour has come back to your cheeks and the light to your eyes. You slept while I guarded you. My eyes were heavy, but I dared not shut them; I watched the folds of your jacket rising and falling, the breath as it came through the arch of your lips; the gold of your curls against the straw; the oval of your cheek and your lashes. My eyes never closed.—I have given up everything for you, Kaya, my life and my art."

He stretched out his arms to her again, and his dark eyes gazed into her blue ones, passionate and eager.

"—Kaya!"

She put out her hand and touched his:

Olive M. Briggs

"Sleep, Velasco. Your life is safe and your art. You have given them to me, but I will give them back again. Break off a piece of the bread, Velasco, and we will talk a little together while we eat. We have been such good comrades, you and I, and we care for one another—as comrades do. If you should die or—or leave me, it would break my heart—you know that."

"Ah, kiss me—Kaya! Let me take you in my arms! Come to me and let me kiss you on your lips!"

"You hurt me, Velasco, your hands are so strong! Not on the lips—Velasco—not on the—lips! I beseech you, dear friend,—I—"

The gypsey held her close to him for a moment, his heart beating against hers, and then he turned away his head. "I love you, Kaya; I love you! Kiss me of your own will. I can't force you—how can I? Your hands are struggling in mine, but they are soft like the down on a bird's breast! Some day you will come to me, Kaya, some day—when you love me too. When—ah! The touch of your hands, your hair against my cheek sets my blood on fire! Feel my pulse how it throbs! It is like a storm under the skin! I suffer, little Bradjaga—little comrade!"

"Don't suffer!" cried the girl, "Let me go, Velasco, let me go! We will sit here together, side by side; be my comrade again, my big brother! Laugh, Velasco! Smile at me! When you look like that and come so close, I am frightened! Don't tease me any more! The bread is hard like a nut; see, I will crack it between my teeth. Where is the honey-cake, Velasco? Give me a piece."

"Do you care for me, Kaya? Look me in the eyes and tell me."

The girl pushed him away from her slowly and turned away her head with a flush: "Is that your violin over there in the straw, lying in a little nest all by itself,—cradled so snug and so warm? It is charming to be a gypsey, Velasco. Are you glad I came to you, or are you sorry? That night, do you remember the violets? I flung them straight at your feet! I wasn't a boy then, but I threw straight. Velasco, listen—I—I care for you—but don't—kiss me!"

"Kaya—Kaya!"

"Hush! Shut your eyes! Put your head back in the straw and go to sleep. When it is time for the dance I will wake you. I will sit here close beside you and watch, as you watched over me. Shut your eyes, Velasco."

"Won't you—Kaya?"

"Go to sleep, Velasco—hush!"

"If I shut my eyes—will you?"

"Hush!"

The sun-beams danced on the dusty floor and the light came dimly through the cobwebs. Velasco lay with his arm under his head, his young limbs stretched in the straw, asleep. He murmured and tossed uneasily. There was a flush on his face; his dark hair fell over his brows and teased him, and he flung it back, half unconscious.

Kaya covered him with the blanket, kneeling beside him in the straw. She moved without rustling, drawing it in softly, and smoothing the straw with her fingers.

"It is my fault that he is lying here in a loft," she whispered low to herself, "He does it for me! His hands have been frozen—for me! They were so white, and firm, and supple; and now—they are scratched and swollen!"

She gave a frightened glance about the loft, and then bent over him, holding back a fold of the blanket.

"He is asleep!" she breathed, "He will never know!"

She stooped low with her golden head and kissed his hands one after the other, lightly, swiftly, pressing her lips to the scratches. He murmured again, tossing uneasily; and she fell backwards in the straw, gazing at him, with her arms locked over her breast and her heart throbbing madly.

"No—he is asleep!" she said, "He is fast asleep! Another hour, and then in the dusk I will wake him. He will play for the dancing—Velasco! The greatest violinist in all Russia— he will play for the peasants to dance!"

She gave a little sob, half smothered. "It was wicked," she said, "unpardonable! I didn't know then—how could I know? If I had known!—God, save him! Give him back his life and his art that he has given to me. Give it all back to him, and let me suffer alone the curse of the Cross—the curse of the— Cross! Make me strong to resist him! Ah, Velasco—!"

She was sobbing through her clenched teeth; staring at him, stretching out her arms to him.

—"Velasco!"

CHAPTER XI

The room was long, and low, and bare, lighted in the four corners by lamps, small and ill-smelling. The ceiling was blackened by the smoke from them, and the air was heavy, clouding the window-panes. At one end of the room was a raised platform, and on the platform sat two gypseys; the one was dark, in a picturesque, tattered costume, with a scarf about his waist, and a violin; the other was slight, with golden curls clipped short, and a ragged jacket of velveteen, worn at the elbows.

The floor of the room was crowded with dancers; sturdy, square-faced moujiks in high boots; and their sweethearts in kerchiefs and short skirts. The moujiks perspired, stamping the boards with their boots until the lamps rattled and shook, and the smoke rolled out of the chimneys; embracing the heavy forms of the women with hands worn and still grimy with toil. The tones of the violin filled the room. "One, two—one, two—one, two, three—curtsey and turn—one, two, three."

The dark haired gypsey sat limply in his chair, playing, his back half turned to the room. There was no music before him. He improvised as he played, snatches of themes once forgotten, woven and bound with notes of his own. His eyes were closed; he swayed a little in his chair, holding the violin close to his cheek.

"One, two—one, two—one, two, three."

The younger gypsey sat cross-legged on the floor, gazing down at the whirling crowd, blurred by the smoke. In his hands he held a tambourine, which he shook occasionally in rhythm with the waltz, glancing over his shoulder at his companion and laughing. Occasionally they whispered together.

"You play too well, Velasco! Hist—scratch with the bow!"

"I can't, Kaya, it is maddening!"

"Just a little, Velasco."

"Is that better? Tysyacha chertei, how it rasps one's ears!"

"Yes, but your technique, Velasco! No gypsey could play like that! Leave out the double stops and the trills!"

"I forget, little one, I forget! The Stradivarius plays itself. Keep the castanet rattling and then I will remember."

"Velasco, hist—st! There are strangers standing by the door; they have just come in! Scratch a little more, just a little. Your tone is so deep and so pure. When you rubato, and then quicken suddenly, and the notes come in a rush like that, I can hardly keep still. My pulses are leaping, dancing! One, two—one, two, three!"

"Is that right? Don't ask me to scratch, Kaya! I can't bear it so close to my ear. The din of their stamping is frightful, the swine! No one will notice."

The whispering ceased. The gypsey bent his dark head again and the violin played on. "One, two—one, two, three!"

All of a sudden, voices began to call out from the floor, here and there among the dancers, irritated and angry; then an oath or two: "Keep time, Bradjaga, keep time!" Their heels beat against the floor.

The landlord crossed the room hastily, edging in and out among the dancers; he was frowning and rubbing his hands one over the other. When he reached the platform, he leaned on it with his elbows and beckoned to the gypsies.

"You don't play badly," he called, "not badly at all; but Dimitri, the old man, he suited them better. He always came strong on the beat. Play the old tunes, Bradjaga; something they know with a crash on the first, like this."

He clapped his hands: "*One*, two, three! *One*, two, three! And fast—just so, all the time!"

"Chort vozmi[1]!" cried Velasco, "They don't like my playing! Don't clap your hands again—don't! The racket is enough to split one's ear-drums!"

He dropped his violin on his knees and stared blinking at the landlord, who was still gesticulating and taking little skipping steps by way of illustration.

"*One*, two, three—*one*, two, three! So, loud and strong! Just try it, Bradjaga!"

Velasco blinked again and a flush came slowly in his cheeks: "My poor Stradivarius," he said slowly in Polish, "They don't like you; they prefer a common fiddler with a crash on the beat! Bozhe moi! Kaya, do you hear?"

The younger gypsey made a sound half startled, half laughing, drawing nearer to him on the platform. "Hist, Velasco! They are peasants; they don't know! Ah, be careful—the strangers are crossing the floor. They are looking at you and talking together! I knew it, I feared it!"

The dancing had stopped, and threading their way through the groups came several ladies and a gentleman.

"Bradjaga," said the landlord, "This is Ivan Petrokoff, the famous musician of Moscow, who has deigned to honour my humble house with his presence. He wishes to examine your instrument."

The gentleman nodded brusquely and stretched out a fat hand. He was short and quite bald, and he stuttered as he spoke. "Quite a d-decent fiddle for a gypsey," he said, "Let me s-see it!"

Velasco bowed with his hand on his heart: "It is mine," he said in a humble voice, "A thousand pardons, Barin! Impossible!"

"I will p-pay you for it!" said the gentleman angrily, "How much do you w-want?"

Velasco smiled and put his hand to his heart again, shrugging his shoulders.

"Not that it is of any p-particular value," continued Petrokoff, "but I like the t-tone. I will give you—hm—s-sixty-five roubles!"

Velasco drew the bow softly over the strings; he was still smiling.

"Seventy! That is exorbitant for a g-gypsey's fiddle! You could buy a d-dozen other instruments for that, just as good! Come—will you t-take it?"

Velasco began to trill softly on the G string, and then swept over the arch with an arpeggio pianissimo.

"You are like a J-Jew!" exclaimed the musician. "You want to bargain! One hundred r-roubles then! There!" He turned to the landlord, stretching out his fat hands, palms upwards. "Absurd isn't it? The f-fellow must be mad!"

"Mad indeed," echoed the landlord, "A miserable, tattered bradjaga, who can't even keep time. You heard yourself, Professor, how he changed the beat and threw the dancers out, every moment or so. They are nothing but tramps; but if you want a fiddle, Barin, old Dimitri, who is sick in bed with the rheumatism in his legs, he will sell you his for a quarter the price and be thankful. A nice little instrument, fine and well polished, not old and yellow with the back worn!"

He twiddled his fingers in contempt.

Velasco ran lightly a scale over the strings. His hair fell over his brows and he half closed his eyes, gazing at the musician through the slits mockingly.

"Are you really the great Petrokoff?" he said, "The Professor of the Violin known through all Russia! From Moscow? Even the gypsies have heard of you!"

The Professor lifted his fingers to his lips and blew on them as if to warm the ends, which were flat and stubbed from much playing on the strings: "Humph!" he said, "You are only a boy! You are talented, it is true; but what do you know of violinists? You ought to be studying."

　　　　　Olive M. Briggs

"That is true, Barin," said Velasco humbly. "I am only a poor gypsey; I know nothing!"

"Let me see your hand and your arm," said Petrokoff, "Yes, the shape is excellent; the muscles are good. You need training of course. If you come to the Conservatory at Moscow, I may be able to procure for you a scholarship for one of my classes."

"Ah, Barin—your Excellence, how kind you are!" murmured the gypsey. "I should like it above all things! Would the Barin teach me himself?"

"Certainly," said Petrokoff loftily, "Certainly; but you would have to pass an examination. Your bowing, for instance, is bad! You should hold your arm so, and your wrist like this."

"Like this?" murmured Velasco, curving his wrist first in one way, then in another. "That is indeed difficult, Barin."

"Give the bow to me," said Petrokoff, "Now, let me show you! I am very particular about that with all my pupils. There—that is better."

The gypsey brushed a lock from his eyes and took up the bow carefully, as if he were handling an egg with the shell broken. "Ah—so?" he said, "Of course! And can you play with your wrist like that, Barin?"

Petrokoff stretched out his hand and took the violin from the gypsey's arms: "Give it to me," he said, "You notice how limpid, how rich the tone! That comes from the method. You will learn it in time; the secret lies in the bowing, the way the wrist is held—so!"

Velasco opened his eyes wide: "Oh, how clumsy I am in

comparison!" he said wistfully. "Your scale, Barin! I never heard such a scale." He gave a swift glance over his shoulder at his companion with a low whistle of astonishment.

"Your comrade seems to be choking," said one of the ladies, "I never heard any one cough so. Is he consumptive?"

"No—no!" said the gypsey. "It is probably a crumb of bread gone the wrong way; or the dust blown about by the dancing. He will recover. Barin—now tell me, do I hold the elbow right?"

"Not at all. The arm must be—so!"

"Ah—so?"

"That is better."

The gypsey ran his fingers over the strings in exact imitation of Petrokoff. The tone was thin, and his fingers moved stiffly as if weighted. His face wore an anxious expression. "Dear me!" he exclaimed, "It is more difficult than I imagined. Does every violinist hold his bow like that?"

Petrokoff cleared his throat and his chest swelled a little under his coat. "Bradjaga, I have taught the violin for twenty-five years—there is no other way."

The gypsey sighed. "My own way is so much simpler," he said, "Look!" His fingers flew over the neck of the Stradivarius in harmonics, swift and sure as the flight of a hawk; his bow seemed to leap in his hand, and when he reached the top note of all, high, clear and sweet, he trilled on it softly, swelling out into a tone pure and strange like the sighing of wind in the tree-tops. The hair fell over his brows, and for a moment there was silence in the room.

Kaya had stopped coughing; she had clapped one hand over her mouth to still the sound, and her blue eyes were fixed on one of the ladies, who was staring hard at the gypsey. They were listening intently. Petrokoff stood with his hands clasped over his waistcoat, his head a little to one side, nodding gently from time to time, as if listening to a pupil in his class room.

"Yes," he began, "as I said before, you have talent. I think I could make something of you; but your bowing is bad, very bad; your method is abominable! It would never be allowed in the Conservatory; and your harmonics—bah!"

He shrugged his shoulders, spreading his fat fingers in disgust. "Give me the violin again; it is too good an instrument for a boy. If you come to Moscow, I will give you two hundred roubles, just out of charity. The instrument isn't worth the half, as you know. But I have a good heart, I am interested in your progress. With the two hundred roubles you can pay for your lodging and food. The harmonics— listen! They should sound like this."

He played a few notes on the top of the instrument, shrill and sharp. The gypsey stretched out his arms eagerly.

"Let me try, Barin!" he cried, "So—so?"

The harmonics seemed to squeak in derision; they flatted, and the sound was like the wheels of a cart unoiled.

"Stop!" cried Petrokoff, "It is horrible! For the love of heaven, Bradjaga, stop!"

The gypsey drew the bow slowly and lingeringly over the flatted notes. It was like the wail of a soul in inferno; a shriek like a devil laughing.

"Ha-ha!" cried Velasco. "Now I understand! That is what you were after, Barin?"

Petrokoff eyed him sharply.

The boy's face was the picture of innocence; the mouth was slightly puckered as if with concentrated effort; his eyes were open and frank; he was smiling a little triumphantly like a child that is sure of pleasing and waiting for praise.

"You play atrociously," said Petrokoff severely. "I shall keep you six months on finger exercises alone. You play false!"

The light died out of the boy's face:

"Barin," he said humbly, "In Moscow you will teach me to play like yourself. I am nothing but an ignorant bradjaga as you see."

Suddenly he put his hand to his mouth and began to cough: "The dust!" he said, "It has gone to my throat all at once. Eh—what? Excuse me a moment, Barin."

Kaya's yellow curls were close to his ear and she whispered something. She was standing behind his chair and, as she stooped to him, her hand rested on his shoulder and trembled slightly: "Velasco," she said, in a voice like a breath, "Come, I beseech you! You are playing with danger, with death! They will surely suspect; ah, come!"

The gypsey tossed his head, like a young horse when some one is trying to force the bit between his teeth; his chin stiffened and an obstinate look came into his eyes. He brushed her aside: "No," he murmured, "Go away, Kaya! He is a stupid fool, can't you see? I am not half through; it is heavenly to hear him! Go—go! I want to tease him some more; I tell you I will."

The younger gypsey sank back on the floor cross-legged, half hidden by the chair and the form of Velasco. Her hands were still trembling and she put them in the pockets of her jacket, trying to force her red lips to a whistle; but no sound came through the arch. She heard the voice of Velasco smooth, and wicked, and humble, just above her.

"There is a musician," he was saying, "Perhaps you have heard of him? His name is Velasco."

"Bosh!" said Petrokoff in an angry tone, and then he blew his nose loudly. "Velasco—bosh! He is only a trickster! There is a fad nowadays among the ladies to run after him." He bowed to the three ladies in turn mockingly, "My friends here tried to get tickets last week in St. Petersburg, but the house was sold out. Bosh—I tell you! I wouldn't cross the street to hear a virtuoso like that!"

The gypsey gave a queer sound like a chuckle: "He does not play as you do, of course, Barin!"

"I!" cried Petrokoff. He twirled his mustache fiercely. "The Russians are like children, they run after every new play-thing. The Pole is a new plaything, a toy—bah! I have been before the public twenty-five years. I am an artist; I am one of the old School. I—"

"Go away, Kaya!" whispered Velasco, "This is grand! I haven't enjoyed myself so much for an age. Go away, little one; don't be frightened. It is all right, only don't cough too much, or the ladies will see you are laughing.

"Ah, Velasco, come—come!"

"Go away, child! He is opening his mouth again, the fat monster! Watch the 'I' leap out! If he plays again I shall die in a fit; he handles the bow like the fin of a shark. Be still, Kaya—go!"

"Velasco—listen, won't you listen? The ladies—ah, don't turn your head away—the one with the grey bonnet is the Countess Galli. I have seen her often at my father's house, Velasco; and she stares first at me, then at you. She suspects."

"The fright, with the long nose?"

"Yes, and the pince-nez."

"She is staring now. Make up a face at her, Kaya; that will scare her away. She has never seen you in boy's clothes before, I warrant, with your hands in your pockets, and your curls clipped short, and a cap on the back of your head—ha ha!"

"Velasco, don't laugh. Don't you see she is whispering to Petrokoff now and looking at us through her pince-nez?"

"So she is, the vixen, the miserable gossip! Slip out towards the door quietly, Kaya, while they are talking. I will follow directly. Wait at the back of the stable by the hay loft."

The gypsey stood up suddenly and approached the little group of ladies, bowing to them and to Petrokoff. He was wrapping the violin in its cover and laying it away in its case as he moved. "Pardon, Barin," he said softly, "If you will wait for me here, I shall return presently. My supper is waiting. Perhaps after an hour you will still like to purchase the violin. See, it is really not a bad instrument—if you are in earnest about the two hundred roubles?"

Olive M. Briggs

Petrokoff stepped eagerly forward. "Now," he said, "Give it to me now. I will hand you the money at once in notes."

"Presently, Barin," said Velasco still softly, "I will return directly. If your Excellency will permit—"

He slipped past the outstretched arm of the musician; bowed again to the lady in the grey bonnet, staring straight into the gold-rimmed lorgnette; and the door closed behind him. Running like a grey-hound, Velasco darted through the corridor and around by the side of the inn to the stable. It was dark there, deserted, and beyond, the snow glittered on the meadows.

"Kaya—are you there?"

"Here, Velasco."

"Have you the knapsack?"

"Yes—yes, here it is."

"Take my hand then and run—run, Kaya, for the Countess has told Petrokoff; she has told him by now. They'll be hot on our tracks! This way—to the left of the road! Hold fast to my hand and run, Kaya—run!"

"I will, Velasco, I will!"

"Don't fall—don't stumble!"

"I won't! Which way? I can't see the road."

"Ahead, straight ahead! Hold me faster! Leap as I leap—and if you hear hoofs, sink down in the shadow."

"Yes—yes, Velasco!"

"Ah, run, dearest—run, for the fiends are behind us! I hear hoofs and bells. Run—run!"

[1] The devil take you.

CHAPTER XII

"Who is in the sleigh, Kaya, can you see? Keep low in the shadow and don't move your head."

"The Countess, Velasco, and Petrokoff and two other men."

"Gendarmes?"

"I think they are gendarmes, Velasco. They look from side to side of the road as they pass and urge the driver forward."

"Bozhe moi, little one! Keep close to me and hold your breath; in another moment they will be past."

"Now—Velasco! Now they are out of sight; the last tinkle of the bells sounds in the distance. Shall we lie here, or follow?"

The gypsey took a long breath and rose to his feet, brushing the snow from his trousers and coat. The girl still sat crouching behind the drift, peering ahead into the dark windings of the road and listening.

"Come, little one!" said Velasco, "The fields are covered deep with the snow; there are no paths and we cannot go back. Give me your hand. You will freeze if you linger."

The girl put her hand in his, springing up, and they darted into the dark windings together, making little rushes forward, hand in hand; then poising on one foot and listening.

"They might turn back you know, Velasco."

"Do you hear the bells?"

"Not yet."

Then they ran on.

The night grew darker and darker; the sky was heavy and black with clouds, and between them a faint light flitted occasionally like the ghost of a moon, but feeble and wan. It struggled with the clouds, piercing them for an instant; and then it was gone and the sky grew blacker, like a great inky; surface, reflecting shadows on the snowfields, gigantic and strange. The wind had died down, but the cold was intense, bitter, and the chill of the ice crept into the bones.

"What is that dark thing ahead on the road, can you see, Velasco?"

"Hist—Kaya, I see! It is big and black. It seems to be a house, or an inn, for look—there are lights like stars just appearing."

"Not that, Velasco, look closer, in front of the house; does it look like a sleigh?"

Velasco's grip tightened on the woolen glove of the girl and they halted together, half hesitating.

"A sleigh, Kaya? Stay here in the shadow—I will steal ahead and look."

"Don't leave me; let me go with you!"

The woolen glove clung to him and they went forward again, a step at a time, with eyes straining through the snow.

"Is it the sleigh of the Countess, big and black with three horses abreast?"

"Yes—it looks so."

"Is there some one inside?"

"The driver perhaps! No, there is no one. Velasco, they have gone into the inn to drink something warm and ask questions perhaps—'Have you seen two gypsies, one dark and one fair?'—Ah, Velasco, what shall we do? Shall we creep past on tiptoe?"

The girl drew close to him and looked up in his face. "What shall we do, Velasco—speak! You stand there with your eyes half shut, in a dream. Shall we run, Velasco? Shall we run on ahead?"

The gypsey put his finger to his lips and crept forward. "This is a God-forsaken hole, Kaya!" he whispered, "No tele-graph—and perhaps no horses; they could only get oxen or mules. It will take several minutes to drink their hot tea—and the brutes are quite fresh!"

He moved cautiously, swiftly, to the hitching post, fumbling with the straps. The horses whinnied a little, nosing one another and pawing the earth.

"What are you doing, Velasco?"

"Jump in, Kaya, jump in—quick, or the driver will hear!

Take the fiddle! Ah, the deuce with this knot!"

With a last tug the knot yielded. Velasco dashed to the step and sprang on it; then his knees gave beneath him, and he fell in the snow as the horses leaped forward.

"Oi—oi! Tysyacha chertei! A pest!"

With oaths and shrieks of rage the driver rushed from the kitchen of the inn, wiping the vodka from his beard with his sleeve. From the tea-room three other men rushed forward, also shouting, and behind them the Countess.

"What is it?" she screamed, "Have the horses run away? Where is the sleigh and my buffalo robe? Are they stolen? Catch the thieves—catch them!"

Velasco still lay in the snow, stunned by his fall, a dark patch like a shadow. The sleigh had turned suddenly and veered around, not half a rod distant. Kaya stood with the reins uplifted, dragging back on the bits; and the horses were rearing, plunging, back on their haunches, slipping on the ice.

"Velasco!" she cried, "Velasco!"

Her voice rang out like a trumpet, echoing over the snow; and as she cried, she swept the horses about and lashed them with the whip, until they came leaping and trembling close to the patch on the snow, which had begun to stir slowly, awaking from the swoon.

"Ah, if I were a man!" she cried, "If I were only a man and could lift you!" She clinched her teeth, swinging the whip, reining back the struggling animals with her slim, white hands from which she had torn the gloves.

Olive M. Briggs

As the figure moved again uneasily, half sitting up in the snow, the men rushed forward.

"Here they are—the gypsies! We have them! They were stealing the sleigh, the rascals!"

As they sprang at Velasco, surrounding him, there came suddenly a swift whizz through the air, a singing as of a hornet, and the heavy lash struck them, across the face, the eyes, the shoulders, stinging and sharp, leaving cruel welts as it struck. The driver screamed out, half blinded. The gendarmes started back. Petrokoff fell on his knees and cowered behind a bush, his fat body trembling and his hands outstretched as if praying:

"For the love of the saints!" he cried, "Don't strike!"

The lash flashed through the air, blinding and terrible in its rapidity. The gypsey leaned over the dash-board, her face white, her eyes dark with rage, her cap on the back of her yellow curls; and the whip seemed to leap between her fingers like something alive.

"Velasco!" she screamed, "Get up! Come—ah, come, while I beat them, the fiends!"

The cry seemed to pierce the benumbed brain of her companion, as the lash the skin. The dark patch moved again and Velasco struggled to his feet; he ran towards the sleigh. The girl leaned forward once more and as the gendarmes sprang towards them again, swearing at her and shouting, she lashed them fiercely across the face and the eyes, mercilessly, with little cries of rage. Velasco tumbled in beside her on the seat.

"Are you there?" she cried, "Are you safe?"

Then she turned, and loosening the reins the lash fell on the horses, cutting them sharply; and they dashed forward, the foam dripping from their bits and their hoofs striking sparks from the ice as they fled, galloping madly, swiftly, through the snow.

In a moment the inn was left behind, the shouting and swearing died away in the distance, and there was silence, broken only by the panting of the horses and the sound of their hoofs galloping. Kaya still urged them forward, shaking the reins in her left hand and lashing with the whip.

"You are safe!" she cried, "You are there, Velasco?"

And then as the silence continued, a great fear came over her; her heart seemed to leap in her throat and her pulses stopped beating. She stooped over him, unheeding the horses. They were in the midst of the forest now, and the next town was several versts distant. It was dark and she put her face close to his, crying out: "Velasco! Velasco!"

Then she saw that he had fainted again; from his forehead a dark stream was gushing slowly; and when she touched it, it was warm and wet. She gave a little cry.

The horses galloped on, but the sleigh moved more smoothly and slid over the icy surface of the snow. Kaya wound the reins about the dash-board. They were quiet now, let them gallop! She bent again over her companion and, taking the snow that lay on the side of the sleigh, she bathed the wound with it, staunching the flow with her handkerchief, holding his head against her breast.

"Velasco!" she whispered low, as if afraid he might waken and hear: "It is better now. The wound has stopped bleeding—only a drop or two comes on my handkerchief!

Olive M. Briggs

You struck it on the runners as you fell; I will bind it now with my scarf. Velasco—dear Velasco! Open your eyes and look at me—smile at me! We are safe. We are alone in the forest and the horses are galloping. Soon we shall be at the station—in the train! A few hours from the frontier—only a few hours—Velasco!"

He stirred in her arms and moaned, and his eye-lids quivered as if trying to open. Kaya took the scarf from her waist and began to wind it slowly about the wound on his forehead. Her breath came in little gasps through her parted lips.

"Have I your blood too on my hands, Velasco? Ah, waken and look at me! We have only a few hours more together—a few hours! Then you will never see me again. Never—never!"

She clasped him closer to her breast and bent over him in terror. "Don't die, Velasco! The wound has stopped bleeding. Why don't you open your eyes? Don't die! If you die I shall die too. I love you, Velasco! I love you—I love you!"

She laid her cheek to his cold one and tried to warm it. She covered him with her cloak. It grew darker and colder, and the horses galloped on. Presently he stirred again in her arms and opened his eyes, and they looked at one another.

"Kaya" he said, "I heard you—I heard you!"

She shrank back away from him: "You heard—me?" she stammered.

Then he fainted again.

The horses galloped on. The fields of snow stretched in the distance, the frost on the surface glittering like myriads of tiny dew-drops. Through the inky blackness of the clouds the moon shone out fitfully, Streaking the road with flashes of light, pale and shadowy. Ahead gleamed the lamps of the station. The hoofs rang on the frozen snow.

Suddenly Velasco lifted his head from the breast of Kaya. He steadied himself and sat upright in the seat. The wound was bound about by the red scarf and his face looked white in the faint moon-beams. There was blood on his jacket and the folds of his vest, and the scarf was spotted with crimson blotches.

He stared straight ahead at the tossing manes of the horses, their galloping bodies, three abreast, plunging and straining in the harness; the reins knotted to the dash-board; the dark, winding road bordered by snow-drifts; the lights in the distance looming nearer, and the bulk of the station. His eyes were shining under the bandage, wide-open beneath the brows.

Kaya drew away from him slowly, burying herself in the corner of the sleigh, drawing the buffalo robe close about her and trembling. The cold was bitter.

He drank in the icy air in long breaths, and it seemed to give him strength, to clear the fumes of the brain. He was like one who has been drowning and is coming to life again gradually. Suddenly he turned and they faced one another. The hoofs rang against the ice, pounding forward; the sleigh was lurching, and the runners slipped and slid in the snow.

"Kaya!"

"Velasco."

He put his arms out and they closed around her; he drew her

Olive M. Briggs

nearer and nearer with all the strength in his body, and she yielded slowly, resisting and weak. She yielded until his lips were on hers, and then she flung out her arms with a little cry and they clung together, closely, silently.

The horses galloped on and the sleigh lurched faster—and faster.

CHAPTER XIII

The night train steamed swiftly through the darkness, the cars swaying from side to side of the track, and the couplings clanging and jolting. It was warm inside the compartments and the air made a thick steam on the windows, hiding the snowfields and the station as the train rushed thundering past. In one of the third-class compartments two gypsies sat together with their heads close to the window, peering out.

"Half an hour now, Velasco."

"Twenty-two minutes, Kaya."

"Now, only twelve."

"Are the passports ready, Velasco?"

"They are here, little one. There is Virballen now in the distance; can you see the roofs and the eagle floating? In another moment, another second—!"

The two gypsies sat quiet, straining their eyes through the steam; then the dark one rose suddenly and adjusted the strap of his knapsack, taking his violin in his hand.

"The train is slowing up now, Kaya, come! Follow me close,

and look neither to the right nor the left."

The two sprang from the train, and hurrying into the customs-room of the station were soon lost in the crowd. The minutes dragged slowly.

"Do you see that paling, Kaya? The other side of it is Germany—is freedom."

"I know, Velasco—I know!"

"Your heart is beating and throbbing, Kaya; your jacket tosses like a ship in a storm. Fold your arms over its fluttering, little one, that the guards may not see. They are coming now."

"Pray—Velasco!"

"To whom should I pray? The Tsar perhaps—or the Icon over yonder?" The gypsey laughed, holding out the pass-ports. He was swaggering with his hands in his pockets, and when the official spoke to him, he shrugged his shoulders and answered in dialect.

"Bohemian!" he said, "Yes—gypsies! We earn our living on the road, my comrade and I—eh, Bradjaga?" With that, he clapped Kaya on the shoulder, showing his white teeth and laughing: "No baggage, Barin, no—no, only this—and that!"

He pointed to the knapsack swung from his shoulder and the violin in his hand.

"What does this ragamuffin do?" demanded the official, looking narrowly at Kaya, "He is fair for a gypsey."

The girl started back for a moment, her shoulder brushing the shoulder of Velasco; then she lifted her blue eyes to the official, and her heart seemed to leap and bound like a wild thing caged. She began to stammer, shrinking back against her companion. A bell sounded suddenly in the office behind them and the official started:

"A telegraph despatch!" he said, "Ha—I must go!"

The girl sprang forward and clutched his sleeve: "Don't go!" she said, "You ask what I can do—I can dance! We will show you, my comrade and I. In a moment the doors will be unlocked; wait until the doors are unlocked! We will give you a performance now, a special performance such as the Tsar himself has heard and seen—Play!"

She waved Her hand to Velasco, and in a moment the violin was out of its wrappings and held to his cheek. He was playing a wild, strange rhythm and Kaya was dancing. The crowd made a circle about them, and the official stood in the centre transfixed, open-mouthed.

The violin was like a creature alive, it sobbed and laughed; and when it sobbed, the little figure of the dancer swayed slowly, languidly, like a flower blown to and fro by the breeze; and when it laughed, the rhythm quickened suddenly in a rush like an avalanche falling, and the figure sprang out into the air, turning, twisting, pirouetting; every movement graceful, intense, full of feeling and passion.

The crowd about the gypsies stood spell-bound; the official never stirred. The bell rang again and again. Every time it rang, a new impetus seemed to seize the dancer. Her feet in the heavy boots seemed scarcely to touch the ground; the green of the velveteen was like the colour of a kaleidoscope, and the gold of her curls glittered and sparkled under the cap. The crowd swayed with the rhythm; they grew drunk with it and their bodies quivered as they watched. The minutes passed like a flash.

Suddenly there came a creak in the lock; the key turned and the great doors opened, the doors towards Germany. Beyond was the long line of paling; the flag with the eagle floating; the sentinels with their muskets over their shoulders. A step and then—

The dancer made a little rush forward, gave a spring in the air and then bowed, snatching off the cap.

"Messieurs—Mesdames!"

She held the cap in her two hands, eagerly, pleadingly, and the silver fell into it. Copecks—ten—twenty—hundreds of them, and roubles, round and heavy; they clinked as they fell.

"I thank you!" cried the gypsey, "Good-bye, Messieurs— Mesdames! Au revoir!"

She bowed again, backing towards the door, the cap still held between her hands, the Violinist following.

"Adieu! Au revoir!"

The crowd clapped noisily, cheering until the great, bare station of the customs rang and re-echoed.

"Au revoir! Adieu!"

The gypsies backed together, smiling, bowing; they passed through the door. They reached the paling—the sentinels; the flag with the eagle floated over their heads; then a click, and the gate closed behind them.

They were on German soil. They were free—they were free.

"Kaya!" said Velasco.

The room at the inn was small and very still. The shades were down, and over in the corner, beyond the couch, a single candle was burning.

"Are you awake, Kaya?" said Velasco softly, bending over the couch until his curls brushed hers, and his lips were close to her rosy cheek.

"I have watched so long for your eyes to open, Kaya! My—wife."

The girl moved uneasily on the pillow.

"My wife—Kaya!"

He put his arms about her and she lay still for a moment, scarcely breathing. Then she spoke:

"I am not your wife, Velasco. Take your arms away."

"Your cheek is so soft, Kaya; the centre is like a red rose blushing. Let me rest my cheek against it."

"Take your cheek away—Velasco."

"Your lips are arched like a bow, so red, so sweet! When I press them—I press—them!"

"Velasco—Velasco! Take your lips—away!"

The girl half rose on her pillow, pushing him back; striking at him feebly with her bare hands; "Go—don't touch me! I have been asleep—I am mad! I am not your wife—Velasco! We must part at once—I tell you, we must part!"

Velasco laughed: "Part!" he said, "You and I, Kaya?—Part? Have you forgotten the church, the priest in his surplice, the dark nave and the candles? We knelt side by side. You are my wife and I am your husband. Kaya, we can never part in life or in death."

The girl put her hand to her breast: "It was only a 'Nihilistic marriage,' Velasco, you know what that means! A mere form for the sake of the certificate, the papers—just to show for the passport that we might go together." Her voice came through her throat roughly as if it hurt her.

Velasco laughed again shortly: "What is that to me?" he said, "We were married; you are my wife. Put your hands down, Kaya—let me take you in my arms. You know—throughout the journey, when we were tramping through the snow and the cold, I treated you as a comrade, for your sake. You asked it. You know—Kaya? And now—now we are in Germany; we are gypsies no longer. You are the Countess and I am Velasco—your husband, Kaya, your—husband."

He stretched out his arms to her, and his eyes were like sparks of light under his brows, gleaming. His hands trembled: "Look at me, Kaya, look at me. Why do you torment me?"

The girl thrust her hand slowly into the breast of her jacket and drew out a paper. "You lost it," she said, "in the prison. I found it on the floor. The—the certificate of our marriage. I swore that night—if we reached the frontier I would— Velasco, don't touch me!—I would destroy it!"

She held it away from him and her eyes gazed into his.

"You would never destroy it, Kaya!" He looked at her and then he gave a cry: "Stop—Kaya!"

She had torn the paper across into strips and was flinging the pieces from her; she was laughing. "You, my husband, Velasco? Are you mad? The daughter of General Mezkarpin marry a musician! Our family is one of the oldest in Russia and yours—!" She laughed again wildly, clasping her hands to her throat. "You are mad—Velasco!"

He looked at her steadily. "Tell me the truth," he said, "Do you love me, or do you not love me? Yes, or no."

"No, Velasco. You were kind to me—you saved my life; I am grateful. If it had not been for you—" Then she laughed again, staggering to her feet. "Love you? No—no! A thousand times—no!"

"That is a lie," said Velasco. "You are trembling all over like a leaf. Your cheeks are ashy. The tears are welling up in your eyes like a veil over the blue. You are breathless—you are sobbing."

He flung his arms around her and pressed her head to his breast, kissing the curls. "Lie still, Kaya, lie still in my arms! The gods only know why you said it, but it isn't the truth! You love me—say you love me! You said it in the sleigh when I was stunned, half conscious! Say it again—Kaya! The certificate is nothing. Does love need a certificate?" He laughed aloud. "Say it, Kaya—let me hear you, my beloved!"

She was silent, clinging to him; she had stopped struggling. Her eyes were closed and he kissed her fiercely on the lips again and again. Presently he was frightened, and a chill of terror and foreboding stole over him.

Olive M. Briggs

"Look at me, Kaya—open your eyes! Have I hurt you—was I too rough? Are you angry? I love you so! The whole world is nothing; art is nothing; fame is nothing. I would sell my Stradivarius for the touch of your fingers in mine, Kaya! I would give my soul for a look in your eyes! Ah, open them—dearest!"

His voice shook and was hoarse, and he held her away from him, gazing down at her face and the panting of her breast. "Tell me you love me—Kaya!"

Suddenly she stiffened until her body was straight and unbending as steel, and the strength came back to her slowly. She opened her eyes and the veil was gone; they were flashing and hard. "You use your strength like a coward, Velasco," she said. "Can you force love? I told you the truth."

She pointed to the fragments of paper on the floor with her finger, scornfully: "There lies the bond between us," she said, "See—it is shattered; it lies at our feet. You will go on your way from here alone, to fill your engagements, and I—" She hesitated and stopped again, as one who is afraid of stumbling.

Her arms stiffened, and her hands, and her whole body; and she drew away from him, avoiding his eyes, and looking only at the fragments of paper on the floor.

"Good-bye now—Velasco," she said.

He looked at her, and he was trembling and shaking from head to foot, like one in a chill. His teeth were clenched and his eyes were bloodshot; the pulses beat in his temples.

"My God!" he cried, "If it is true—if you don't love me! If—"

Kaya stretched out her hand to him, catching her breath. "Good-bye, Velasco—"

He turned on her fiercely, and raised his arm as if he would have struck her: "You are cruel!" he said, crying out, "You are not a woman!" He caught her by the shoulders and held her, looking down into her eyes, with his face close to hers.

"Swear it!" he cried, "Swear it if you can—if you dare! Swear you don't love—me."

She looked at him and her lips trembled.

"Swear it!"

She nodded.

A cry burst from his throat, like that of an animal, wounded, at bay. His blood-shot eyes stared at her for a moment, and then he flung her from him with all his strength and turning, dashed from the room.

The door slammed.

The girl reeled backward, putting her hands to her face. Then, as the echo of his footsteps died away on the stairs, she fell on her knees, crouching and sobbing.

"He is gone!" she cried out, the words coming in little moans through her clenched teeth. "He is gone! Velasco is gone!"

Her form shook in a torrent of weeping, and she took her hands from her face and wrung them together. "I love him!" she said, "I love him! If he had stayed! No—no, I am mad! I am cursed—cursed by the Black Cross. There is blood on my hands!"

Olive M. Briggs

She held them out before her, and they trembled and shook. "Blood!" she cried, "I see it—red—dripping! It fell from his wound on my hand and nothing will wash it away! Nothing!" Her voice died away to a whisper and she knelt, staring at her hands with eyes wild and dilated:

"Not even his love," she said, "not even his love could wash it away. It would spread—he too would be cursed. He—too!" Then she flung herself on the floor and buried her head against the side of the couch, clinging to it, with her body convulsed:

"Come back, Velasco!" she stammered, "I am weak—come back! Put your arms around me—kiss me again! Don't be angry. Don't look at me like that! Velasco—I won't leave you! I—I love you! Come back!"

She lay still, shuddering.

Outside, in the street, came the clatter of wheels passing and the cries of a street vendor; far off came the whistle of a locomotive. Kaya dragged herself to her feet slowly, stumbling a little. She passed her hands over her eyes once or twice, as if blinded; then feebly, like one who has just recovered from a long illness, she tottered towards the door and opened it.

Her head was bare and her curls covered it in a tangle of gold; her jacket and trousers were old and faded, patched at the elbows, torn at the knees. The tears had dried on her cheeks. She gazed ahead steadily without looking back; and the blue of her eyes was like the blue of the sky at night-fall, darkened and shadowy.

At the bend of the stairway she stumbled, half falling; then she steadied herself, clinging to the balustrade with her hands—and went on.

It was day-light, and the cocks were all crowing when Velasco returned. When he opened the door the candle burned low in its socket, and the sun-rays came filtering in through the windows. The room was deserted. He was muddy and footsore; his face looked haggard and old, and it was lined with deep furrows. His dark eyes were listless and weary, and his cheeks colourless.

"Kaya," he said, "are you here? Kaya!"

He looked on the couch, but it was empty; behind the curtains, but there was nothing; out of the windows, but there was only the street below. His eyes had a dazed look.

"Kaya!" he cried.

On the floor lay a boy's cap, torn, rakish, faded with the sun and the snow of their wanderings—a little, green cap. Velasco stared at it for a moment.

Then suddenly he snatched it to his lips with a sob, and buried his head in his arms.

PART II

CHAPTER XIV

Ehrestadt lies in a plain.

The walls of the old city have been leveled into broad promenades, shaded with nut-trees, encircling the town as with a girdle of green. Beyond, a new city has sprung up, spreading like a mushroom; but within the girdle the streets are narrow and crooked, and the houses gabled; leaning to one another as if seeking support for their ancient foundations, with only a line of sky in between.

At the corner of the promenade, just where the old city and the new city meet, is a tumble-down mill. It is called the Nonnen-Muehle, and it has been there ever since Ehrestadt first came into existence, as is evident from the bulging of the walls, and the wood of the casements, rotten and worm-eaten. The river winds underneath it, and the great spoked wheel turns slowly, tossing the water into a cloud of yellow foam, flinging the spray afar into the dark, flowing stream, catching it again; playing with it, half sportive, half fierce, like some monster alive.

As the wheel turns, the sound of its teeth grinding is steady and rhythmical, like a theme in the bass; and the river splashes the accompaniment, gurgling and sighing in a minor key, as if in complaint.

It was Johannestag.[1]

The citizens of Ehrestadt were walking on the promenade, dressed in their best; the men strutting, the women hanging on their arms, the children toddling behind. In the square a band was playing; the nut trees were in full leaf, and the air was warm and sweet with the scent of the rose buds. The wheel of the mill had stopped.

Just under the peak of the roof was a small window gabled, with a broad sill, and casements that opened outwards, overlooking the promenade. The sill was scarlet with geraniums, and the window itself was grown partly over and half smothered in a veiling of ivy. Behind the window was a garret, small like a cell; the roof sloping to the eaves.

There was nothing in the garret excepting a pallet-bed in the corner, under the eaves, and in the opposite corner a box on which stood a pitcher and basin; the basin was cracked; the pitcher was without a handle. On the wall hung a few articles of clothing on pegs; and the slope of the roof was grey and misty with cob-webs. Otherwise the garret was bare.

Sitting by the window with her elbows on the sill, framed by the ivy and the geraniums, was a girl. Her head was propped in her hands, and her hair glittered gold in the warm sunlight against the green and the scarlet. She was gazing eagerly over the throngs on the promenade, and her blue eyes were alert as if searching for some one.

She was young and slim, and her gown was shabby, turned back at the throat as if she suffered from the heat; and her hair was cropped, lying in little tendrils of gold on her neck,

Olive M. Briggs

curling thickly about her ears and her brow. Her cheeks were quite pale, and there was a pinched look about the lips, dark shadows under the eyes. She gazed steadily.

"If I could only see him," she murmured to herself, half aloud, "just once—if I could see him!" Her lip trembled a little and she caught it between her teeth: "It is seventeen weeks—a hundred and nineteen days—since we parted," she said, "At daybreak on Thursday it will be a third of a year—a third of a year!"

She moved her head uneasily on her hands, and hid her eyes for a moment against the leaves of the ivy, as if blinded by the sun-beams; "Sooner or later he was sure to come here," she murmured, "All musicians come here; but when I saw his face on the bill-board to-day—and his name—!" She crouched closer against the sill, and the leaves of the ivy fluttered from the hurried breath that came through her lips, shaking them as with a storm.

"If he were there on the promenade," she said, "and I saw him walking, with his violin, his head thrown back and his eyes dreaming—Ah!" She drew in her breath quickly and a little twist came in her throat, like a screw turned. She half closed her eyes.

"Ah—Velasco! My arms would go out to you in spite of my will; my lips would cry to you! I would clinch my teeth—I would pinion my arms to my side. I would hide here behind the casement and gaze at you between the leaves of the geraniums—and you would never know! You would never—know!"

She put both hands to her bare throat as if to tear something away that was suffocating, compelling; then she laughed: "He is an artist," she said, "a great musician, feted, adored;

he is rich and happy. He will forget. Perhaps he has forgotten already. It would be better if he had forgotten—already." She laughed again strangely, glancing about the garret with its low eaves, and the cob-webs hanging; at the pallet, and the cracked basin, and the pitcher with its handle missing.

The doves came flying about the mill, twittering and chirping as if seeking for food on the sill; clinging to the ivy with their tiny, pink claws, looking at her expectantly out of their bright, roving eyes, pruning their feathers. The girl shook her head:

"I have nothing for you," she said, "No—not a crumb. The last went yesterday. Poor birds! It is terrible to be hungry, to have your head swim, and your limbs tremble, and the world grow blind and dim before your eyes. Is it so with you, dear doves?"

She rose slowly and a little unsteadily, crossing the garret to the pegs where the clothes hung.

"There may be a few Pfennigs left," she said, "without touching that. No—no, there is nothing!"

She felt in the pockets of the cloak, pressing deep into the corners with the tips of her fingers, searching. "No," she repeated helplessly, "there is—nothing; still I can't touch the other—not to-day! I will go out and try again."

She took down the cloak from the peg and wrapped it about her, in spite of the heat, covering her throat. There was a hat also on the peg; she put it on, hiding her yellow curls, and drew the veil over her face.

"If I could only get a hearing!" she said to herself, "There must be someone in Ehrestadt, who would listen to my voice and give me an opening. I will try once more, and then—"

She buttoned the cloak with her fingers trembling, and went out.

"Is the Herr Kapellmeister in?"

"Yes, Madame."

The rosy cheeked maid hesitated a little, and her eyes wandered doubtfully from the veil to the cloak and the shabby skirt.

"Kapellmeister Felix Ritter, I mean."

"He is in, Madame, but he is engaged."

"May I come in and wait?"

The maid hesitated again: "What name shall I say, Madame?"

"My name," said Kaya, "is Mademoiselle de—de Poussin."

The German words came stumbling from her lips. She crossed the threshold and entered a large salon, divided by curtains from a room beyond. There was a grand piano in the corner of the salon, and about the walls were shelves piled high with music; propped against the piano stood a cello.

Kaya looked at the instrument; then she sank down on the divan close to the piano, and put out her fingers, touching it caressingly. From the next room, beyond the curtain, came the sound of cups rattling, and a sweet, rich aroma as of coffee, mingling with the fragrance of cigars freshly lighted.

The girl threw back her veil, scenting it as a doe the breeze when it is thirsty and cannot drink. She smiled a little, still caressing the keys with her fingers. "It is strange to be hungry," she said, "The Countess Mezkarpin was never hungry!" Then suddenly she started and turned white to the lips, swaying forward with her eyes dilated.

From behind the curtain came voices talking together; one was harsh and rather loud, and the other—Kaya's eyes were fixed on the curtain; she rose slowly from the divan and crept forward on tip-toe, a step at a time. The other!—She listened. No, it was the harsh voice talking rapidly, loudly in German, and what he was saying she could not understand; then came the clatter of cups again, and silence, and a fresh whiff of cigar smoke floating, wafted through the curtain.

She crept closer, still listening, her hands clasped together, the cloak flung back from her shoulders.

"The other—there!"

She put out her hand and touched the curtain, pulling it aside slightly, timidly, and pressing her face, her eyes to the opening. She was faint for a moment and could see nothing; there was a mist before her eyes and the smoke filled the room; then gradually, out of the mist, she saw a grey-haired man with his back to the curtain, and he was bending forward with a coffee cup to his lips. Beside him, facing her, leaning far back in his chair, with his cigar poised and his eyes half closed, his dark head pressing restlessly against the cushion was—

"Oh, my God!" she breathed, "My God, it is Velasco!"

For a moment she thought she had screamed; and she covered her eyes waiting, sick, frightened, her heart throbbing. Then she forgot where she was and thought only of him, and a strange little thrill went over her; she shivered slightly, and it seemed to her as if already she was in his arms; and when she heard his voice, it was calling to her, crying her name.

"Yes—yes, it is Kaya!—I am here!" she was saying, "Come to me—Velasco! Velasco!"

Already she was stumbling into his arms; she was clinging to him—and then she awoke. Her brain cleared suddenly and she knew that she had not moved; no sound had come from her lips. She was standing like a statue, dumb, with her hands clasped, gazing; and Velasco lay back in his chair with his eyes half closed, blowing a wreath from his cigar, watching it idly as it floated away, listening as the harsh voice of his host talked on—not five feet away! If she stretched out her hand, if she sighed—or moved the curtain—Ah!

She struggled with herself. She was faint; she was weak with hunger; she was alone and desolate—and he loved her. She fought madly, desperately. It was as if two creatures were within her fighting for life; and they both loved him.

When the one grew stronger, her eyes brightened and her pulses quickened; it was as if she would leap through the curtain, and her heart was sick for the touch of his hand. Then she beat down the longing and stifled it, and the other self came to the front and gripped her scornfully, pointing to her hands with the blood on them, her soul with its curse. Was her life to mingle with his and ruin it, and bring it to shame?

"Never," she breathed, "Never! So long as I live!" And the self of her that loved him the most crushed the other self and smothered it—strangled it.

She gazed at him through the curtain, and it seemed to her that something within her was gasping and dying. And suddenly she turned and ran from the curtain, clasping her cloak to her bosom and running, stumbling, out of the room, the house, the street.

The promenades were gay with people and crowded. The men strutting along in their Sunday clothes, the women hanging on their arms, the children toddling behind. The band was playing on the square. It was warm and the sun was shining; the air was sweet with the scent of the rose buds.

Kaya fled past them all like a wraith. They turned and stared after her, but she was gone. She climbed the stairs of the mill to the roof, and opened the door, and shut it again, and fell on her knees before the box. The pitcher was there without a handle, and the basin cracked. She lifted them away and opened the box.

In it lay a velveteen jacket folded, a scarf, scarlet and spotted. Inside the scarf lay a mass of coins, copecks, ten, twenty—hundreds of them, and roubles round and heavy. She fingered them tenderly, one after the other, then thrust them aside.

"To-morrow—" she said, "I have come to that—to live on a gypsey's wages! I can sing no longer; I can only dance and pass the cap—and give the copecks for bread—for bread! I thought some day when I was old,—when we were both old, I would show them to—Velasco, and he would remember and laugh: 'Ah, that was long ago,' he would say, 'when I was a boy, and you were a boy, and we tramped together through the cold and the snow—and I loved you, and you—loved

Olive M. Briggs

me! Ah—it was sweet, Kaya! I have lived a long life since then, with plenty of fame, and success, and happiness—and the years have been full; but nothing quite so sweet as that! Nothing—quite so sweet—as that!'"

She was sobbing now and staring into the box: "To-morrow," she said, "I will buy some bread and feed the doves—and soon it will be gone!" She began to count the coins rapidly, dropping them through her fingers into the scarf; and as she counted she smiled through her tears.

"We earned it together—he and I!" she said, "He played and I danced. He would like me to live on it as long as I can, and then—after that—he will not—blame me!"

Her body swayed slightly and she fell forward against the box. The sun shone on the geraniums; and on the sill, the doves pecked at the worm-eaten casement, clinging to the ivy with their tiny claws, gazing about with their bright, roving eyes and cooing.

Below, the water splashed against the wheel; but it was silent.

[1] St. John's day.

CHAPTER XV

The stage of the Opera House was crowded with the chorus. It was ten o'clock in the morning, but the day was rainy and the light that came from the windows at the back of the proscenium was feeble and dim, and the House itself was quite dark. The seats stretched out bare and ghostly, row after row; and beyond a dark cavern seemed yawning, mysterious and empty, the sound of the voices echoing and resounding through spaces of silence.

In the centre of the stage stood the Conductor, mounted on a small platform with his desk before him; and around him were the chorus, huddled and watchful as sheep about a shepherd. He was tapping the desk with his baton and calling out to them, and the voices had ceased.

"Meine Herren—meine Damen!" he cried, "How you sing! It is like the squealing of guinea-pigs—and the tenors are false! Mein Gott! Stick to the notes, gentlemen, and sing in the middle of the tone. There now, once more. Begin on the D."

Kapellmeister Ritter glanced over his chorus with a fierce, compelling motion of his baton. He was like a general, compact and trim of figure with a short, pointed beard, and hair also short that was swiftly turning to grey. The only thing that suggested the musician was the heaviness and

Olive M. Briggs

swelling of his brows, and the delicacy of his hands and wrists, which were white, like a woman's, of an extraordinary suppleness and full of power; hands that were watched instinctively and obeyed. The eyes of the entire chorus were fixed on them now, gazing as if hypnotized, and hanging on every movement of his beat.

"Na—na!" he cried, "Was that F, I ask you? You bellow like bulls! Again—again, I tell you! On the D and approach the note softly.

"Hist-st!—Pianissimo!"

He stamped his foot in vexation and the baton struck the desk sharply: "Again—the sopranos alone! Hist! Piano—piano I say! Potztausend!"

The chorus glanced at one another sheepishly and a flush crept over the faces of the sopranos. The Kapellmeister was in a bad mood to-day; nothing suited him, and he beat the desk as if he would have liked to strike them all and fling the baton at their heads.

"Sheep!" he said, "Oxen—cows! You have no temperament, no feeling—nothing—nothing! Where are your souls? Haven't you any souls? Don't you hear what I say? Piano! P-i-a-n-o! When I say piano, do I mean forte?"

He shrugged his shoulders, and his eyes flashed scornfully over the stage and the singers. "Now ladies, attention if you please! Look at me—keep your eyes on my baton! Now—piano!"

The voices of the sopranos rose softly.

"Crescendo!" They increased.

"Donnerwetter! May the devil take you! Crescendo, I say! Crescendo! Do you need all day to make crescendo?" He shrieked at them; and then, in a tempest of rage, he flung the baton down and leaped from the platform.

"Enough!" he said, "My teeth are on edge; my ears burn! Sit down.—Is Fraulein Neumann here?"

A stout woman in a red blouse stepped timidly forward.

"Oh, you are, are you? Well, Madame, you haven't distinguished yourself so far; perhaps you will do better alone. Have you the score?"

"Yes, Herr Kapellmeister."

"Begin then."

The soprano took a long breath and her cheeks grew red like her blouse. She watched the eyes of the leader, and there was a light in them that she mistrusted, a reddish glimmer that boded evil to any who crossed him.

She began tremulously.

"Stop."

She started again.

"Your voice quavers like a jews'-harp. What's the matter with you?"

"I don't know, Herr Kapellmeister, it was all right when I tried it this morning."

"Well, it's all wrong now."

The soprano bit her lips: "I am doing my best, Herr Kapellmeister," she said, "It is very difficult to take that high A without the orchestra." Her tone was slightly defiant, but she dropped her eyes when he stared at her.

"Humph!" he said, "Very difficult! You expect the orchestra to cover your shake I suppose. Go home and study it, Madame. Siegfried would listen in vain for a bird if you were in the flies. He would never recognize that—pah!" He waved his hand:

"Where is the Fraulein who wanted her voice tried?" he said curtly, "If she is present she may come forward." He took out his watch and glanced at it. "The chorus may wait," he said, "Look at your scores meanwhile, meine Herren, meine Damen—and notice the marks!

"Ah, Madame."

A slim figure with a cloak about her shoulders, bareheaded, approached from the wings; her curls, cut short like a boy's, sparkled and gleamed. The Kapellmeister surveyed her coldly as she drew nearer, and then he turned and seated himself at the piano.

"Your voice," he said shortly, "Hm—what?"

"Soprano, Monsieur."

"We have enough sopranos—too many now! We don't know what to do with them all."

The girl shivered a little under the cloak.

"Oh!" she faltered, "Then you won't hear me?"

"I never said I wouldn't hear you, Madame; I simply warned you. If you were alto now—but for a soprano there is one chance in a thousand, unless—" He struck a chord on the piano.

The chorus sat very still. The trying of a new voice was always a diversion; it was more amusing to watch the grilling of a victim than to be scorched themselves; and the Kapellmeister in that mood—oh Je! They smiled warily at one another behind their scores, and stared at the slight, girlish figure beside the pianoforte.

She was stooping a little as if near-sighted, looking over the shoulder of the Conductor at the music on the piano rack.

"Can you read at sight, Madame?"

"Yes," said Kaya.

"Have you ever seen this before?"

"I studied it—once."

"This?"

"I studied that too."

"So," he said, "Then you either have a voice, or you haven't, one or the other. Where did you study?"

The girl hesitated a moment; then she bent lower and whispered to him: "St. Petersburg, Monsieur, with Helmanoff."

"The great Helmanoff?"

"Yes, Monsieur."

Olive M. Briggs

"You are not French then, you are Russian? They told me Mademoiselle Pou—Pou—"

"That is not my real name."

"No?"

Kaya quivered a moment: "I am—Russian," she said, "I am an exile. Don't ask, Monsieur—not here! I am—I am afraid."

The Kapellmeister went on improvising arpeggios on the piano as if he had not heard. He seemed to be pondering. "That name—" he said, "Pou—Poussin! Someone called on me the other day of that name. I remember it, because when I came in she was gone. Was it you?"

The girl stood silent.

He turned suddenly and looked at her: "You are young," he said, "and too slim to have a voice. Na—child! You are trembling as if you had a chill, and the House is like an oven. Come—don't be frightened. The chorus are owls; they can stare and screech, but they know nothing. Sit down here by me and sing what you choose. Let your voice out."

"Shall I sing a Russian song, Monsieur?"

"Very well."

The Kapellmeister leaned back in his chair with his arms folded. He gave one fierce glance at the chorus over his shoulder. "Hush!" he cried, "No noise if you please. Attend to your scores, or go out. Now, Fraulein—sing."

Kaya pushed the chair to one side and moved closer to the piano, leaning on it and gazing out into the darkened House, at the rows of seats, ghostly and empty, and the black cave beyond. A Volkslied came to her mind, one she had heard as a child and been rocked to, a peasant song, simple and touching. Her lips parted slightly.

For a moment there was silence; then the tones came like a breath, soft and pianissimo, clear as the trill of a bird in the forest wooing its mate. It rose and fell, swelling out, filling the spaces, echoing through the vault.

"On the mountain-top were two little doves;
Their wings were soft, they shimmered and shone.
Dear little doves, pray a prayer—a prayer
For the son of Fedotjen, Michaeel—Michaeel,
For he is alone—alone."

With the last word, repeated, half whispered, the voice died away again; and she stood there, still leaning against the piano and clasping her hands, looking at the Kapellmeister with her blue eyes dark and pleading, like two wells. "Will it do?" she said with her voice faltering, "Will you take me, Herr Director—in the chorus?"

The Kapellmeister shrugged his shoulders: "You have no voice for a chorus," he said roughly, "Try this."

"I know," said Kaya, "My voice is not as it was. Helmanoff—" she laughed unsteadily, "He would be so angry if he heard me, and tell me to study, just as you told the Mademoiselle who went out; but I will do better, Monsieur, believe me. I will work so hard, and my voice will come back in time after—" She gazed at him and a mist came over her eyes. "Do take me," she said, "I beg you to take me—I beg you."

The Kapellmeister passed his hand over his face: "Tschut,

Olive M. Briggs

child!" he said, "What are you talking about? Be quiet now and sing this as I tell you. You have heard it before?"

"Yes, I have heard it."

"And sung it perhaps with Helmanoff?"

"Yes—Monsieur."

He handed her the score, running his fingers over the bird motive of 'Siegfried,' giving her the key. Then he leaned back again and folded his arms.

Kaya gave her head a little backward movement as if to free her throat, and threw off the cloak, standing straight.

The tones came out like the sound of a flute, high and pure; they rose in her throat, swelling it out as she sang, pouring through the arch of her lips without effort or strain.

"Bravo!" cried the Director, "Um Himmel's Willen, child, you have a voice like a lark rising in the meadows, and you sing—Bravo! Bravo!"

He put out his hands and took the girl's trembling ones into his own.

"You will take me?" she said, "You see, when I am not so nervous it will go better."

The Kapellmeister laughed and took a card out of his pocket: "Write your name here," he said, "Your real one. I won't tell—and your address."

Kaya drew back suddenly: "I live in the mill," she said, "You know, the Nonnen-Muehle by the promenade? You won't let any one know, will you, Monsieur, because—"

"Are you afraid of spies, child? Tut, the chorus can't hear. I won't tell a soul."

"No one?"

"On my honour—no one. Now, your name?"

She looked away from him a moment; then she took the pencil and wrote on the card in small, running letters: "Marya Pulitsin."

"So that's your real name, is it?"

Her eyes were clear and blue like a child's. "No," she said, "—no." And she glanced back over her shoulder with her finger to her lips.

"Never mind," said the Kapellmeister. "You are white, child, what are you afraid of? There are no spies here! Give me the card. That is a strange place to live in—the Nonnen-Muehle! I didn't know anyone lived there, excepting the old man who takes charge of the mill. Well, in a day or so—perhaps towards the end of the week you will hear from me." He waved to the chorus.

"Stand up, meine Herren, meine Damen!" he said, "Get your scores ready. Good-bye now, Fraulein.—Donnerwetter! What ails you?"

"If you want to try my voice again," said Kaya timidly, "Would you mind, sir, trying it to-day?—This afternoon, or even this evening?"

"Now by all that is holy, why, pray? I have the solos

to-night, and this afternoon a rehearsal for 'Siegfried.'" The Kapellmeister frowned: "Do you think I have nothing on earth to do, child, but run after voices?"

"Oh!" cried Kaya, "I didn't mean that! I beg your pardon. It doesn't matter—I do beg your pardon, Herr Director." She flushed suddenly, and started away from him, as if to put the piano between them and flee towards the door.

He looked at her narrowly, and the harsh lines came back to his face. "A pest on these singers!" he muttered under his breath, "They are all alike—they want coddling. She thinks perhaps she is a Patti and is planning for her salary already. Potztausend! Bewahre!" He turned on his heel curtly and mounted the platform, taking up the baton.

"Now," he cried, "The D again—all together! Pia—no!"

Kaya stole across the stage swiftly on tiptoe, threading her way through the scenery that was standing in rows, one behind the other, in readiness for the performance that night, and disappeared into the wings. It was dusty there and deserted. An occasional stage-hand hurried by in the distance bent on some errand, and from the back came the sound of hammering. The chorus was singing forte now, and the sound filled the uttermost corner, drowning the noise of the hammer. Kaya stood still for a moment, clinching her hands: "My God," she said, "I have tried the last and it has failed! The end of the week!" she laughed to herself bitterly. "I know what that means. Helmanoff used to get rid of new pupils that way: 'You will hear,' he would say; but they never heard."

She took a coin out of her dress and looked at it. "The gypsies' wages are gone," she said, "Only this left to pay for my roof and my bed!" She laughed again and glanced about her stealthily as if fearful of being seen, or tracked. Then she began to breathe quickly:

"*Without weakness,*" she said, "*without hesitation, or mercy, by mine own hands if needs be.* I have done it to another: I will do it again—to myself. Atone, atone—wipe out the stain! A life for a life! That is right." She swayed and caught one of the scenes for support. "That is—just! God, how my throat burns, and my head, it is dizzy—and my eyes have gone blind! Ah, it is passing—passing! Now I can see. I can—walk!"

She clung to the scenery for another second, and then pushed it away and moved to the door, staggering a little like one who is drugged.

It was evening. The rain had ceased, and the moon rose full and pale with a halo about it. In the distance clouds were gathering, and the waters under the mill were speckled with light.

Kaya sat by the window, leaning on the sill with her arms and gazing down at the wheel: "It is deep there," she said, "A moment of falling through the air—a splash, and it will be over. I am not—afraid."

She shuddered a little, and her eyes were fixed on the flashes of silver as if fascinated. She could not tear them away. "How black it is under the wheel!" she murmured, "If I fell on the spokes—" Then she shuddered again.

"Perhaps I shall not die," she said, "Perhaps I shall live and be crippled, with my body broken. Oh, God—to live like that! I must—I must aim for the pool beyond, where the water lies deep and the moonlight freckles the—surface."

Olive M. Briggs

Then she dropped her head on her arms and the words came again: "I have tried my best, Velasco, but the heart is gone out of me. Don't be angry and call me a coward. I tried—but I am weak now and I am afraid. My voice is gone, and there is so little for a woman to do. I tried everything, Velasco, but my strength—is—failing. If I could walk, I would go to you and say good-bye; but I don't know where you are. They say you have gone and I don't know where."

She leaned a little further forward on the sill, still hiding her eyes. "He won't know," she whispered under her breath, "He will never know. Velasco! Velasco—good-bye."

Her body lay across the sill now, and she opened her heavy lids and gazed downwards, half eagerly, half fearfully. The water was dark and the moon-light on the surface glittered. The wheel was below, huge and gaunt like a spectre; silent, with its spokes dipping into the pool.

CHAPTER XVI

"Fraeulein, Fraeulein—open the door! There is a gentleman here who would speak with you!—Fraeulein!"

The blows redoubled on the stout oak, growing louder and more persistent. "Fraeulein! It is very strange, Herr Kapellmeister. I saw her go in with my own eyes, some two hours back, and she has not come out, for I was below in the mill with my pipe and my beer, sitting in the very doorway itself, and no flutter of petticoats passed me, or I should have heard."

The old miller rubbed his wizen cheeks and smoothed the wisps of hair on his chin, nervously as a young man does his mustache.

"Na—!" said the Kapellmeister. "It is late and she may be asleep. I came after rehearsal and it must be nine, or past. Knock louder!"

The miller struck the oak again with his fist, calling out; and then they both listened. "There is no light through the key-hole," said the miller, peeping, "only the moon-rays which lie on the floor, and when I hark with my hand to my ear, I hear no sound but the water splashing."

The Kapellmeister paced the narrow corridor impatiently. "Donnerwetter!" he exclaimed, "The matter is important, or I shouldn't have come. I must have an answer to-night. Try the door, and if it is unlocked, open it and shout. You have a voice like a saw; it would raise the dead."

The miller put his hand to the latch and it yielded: "Fraeulein—!" The garret was in shadow, and across the floor lay the moonbeams glittering; the casement was open, and the geraniums were outlined dark against the sky, their colour dimmed.

"There is something in the window!" said the miller, peering; and the door opened wider. "There is something black across the sill; it is lying over the geraniums and crushing them, and it looks like a woman! Jesus—Maria!"

He took a step forward, staring: "It is the Fraeulein, and she is—"

"Get out of the way, you fool!" cried the Kapellmeister sharply, and he pushed the man back and strode forward: "The child has fainted! She lies here with her head on her arms, and her cheek is white as the moon itself."

He lifted her gently and put his arm under her shoulders, supporting her: "Get some Kirsch at once," he cried to the miller, "Stop gaping, man! She's not dead I tell you—her heart flutters and the pulse in her wrist is throbbing!" He slipped his hand in his pocket, and tossed the miller a gulden. "Now run," he said, "run as if the devil were after you. The Rathskeller is only a square away! Brandy and food—food, do you hear?"

The old man caught the gulden greedily between his fingers, and examined it for a moment, weighing it. "I will go," he mumbled, "certainly I will go. Kirsch—you say, sir, and bread perhaps?"

"Be off, you fool!"

The Kapellmeister watched the door grimly as it shut behind the miller, and then he glanced about the garret. "Poor," he said, "Humph! A place for a beggar!" His eyes roved from the pallet in the corner to the pitcher and the basin, the clothes on the pegs, the cobwebs hanging, the geraniums crushed on the sill.

Then he lifted the girl's head and held it between his hands, looking down at her face, supporting her in his arms. The lashes lay heavy on her cheeks and the tendrils of hair, curly and golden, lay on her neck and her forehead. Her throat was bare; it was white and full. The Kapellmeister held her gently and a film came over his eyes as he gazed:

"How young she is!" he murmured, "like some beautiful boy. Her chin is firm—there is will power there. Her brows are intelligent; her whole personality is one of feeling and temperament. It is a face in a thousand. What is her name, her history? How has she suffered? Why is she alone? There are lines of pain about the mouth—the eyes!"

He raised her suddenly in his arms and started to his feet; and as he did so, she opened her lids slowly and gazed at him. "Velasco—" she murmured.

Her voice was low and feeble, and the Kapellmeister bent his head lower: "What is it, child?" he said, "I can't hear you. In a moment you will have some brandy in your throat and that will rouse you. I will carry you now to that pallet over yonder, a poor place, no doubt, and hard as a board."

He strode across the floor and laid the girl gently on the bed, smoothing the pillow, and covering her lightly with the blanket. Kaya opened her eyes again, and put out her hands as if seeking someone.

"I was falling," she said, "Why did you bring me back?"

The Kapellmeister sat down by the edge of the bed and began to whistle softly; he whistled a theme once, and then he repeated it a semi-tone higher. "I suspected as much," he said, "Was it because you had no money?"

Kaya turned her face away.

"Were you starving?—Tschut! You needn't answer. Your eyes show it. I might have seen for myself this morning, if I had not been in a temper with the chorus, and my mind absorbed in other matters. Be still now, here is the miller—the dotard!"

The Kapellmeister went over to the door, and took from the old man a small flask and a newspaper wrapping some rolls. "So," he said grimly, "Now go, and keep the rest of the gulden for yourself. No thanks! Pischt—be off! Go back to your doorway and finish your beer, do you hear me? I will look after the Fraeulein; she is conscious now, and I have business with her." He motioned the old man back from the door and closed it behind him; then he returned to the pallet. "I'm not much of a nurse," he said, "You will have to put up with some awkwardness, child; but there—raise your head a little, so—and lean on my shoulder! Now drink!"

Kaya swallowed a few drops of the brandy. "That is enough," she said faintly.

"No.—Drink!"

He held the glass to her lips, and she obeyed him, for his hands were strong and his eyes compelled her. Then he broke the roll, and dipped it into the brandy, and fed her piece by piece. When she tried to resist him, he said "Eat, child—eat! Do as I tell you—eat!" and held it to her mouth until she yielded.

She thought of Velasco and how he had fed her in the studio, and the pulse in her wrist beat quicker. When she had finished the roll, he put down the glass and the newspaper, and she felt his eyes searching hers, keen and sharp, two daggers, as if they would pierce through her secret.

"Don't speak," he said curtly, "Listen to me and answer my questions: Why were you discouraged? I told you this morning you would hear from me; why didn't you wait?"

The tears rose slowly into Kaya's eyes, and she hid her face in the pillow.

"You didn't believe me," said the Kapellmeister, "but you see I was better than my word—I have come myself. Why do you suppose I have come?"

She lay silent.

"If I hadn't come," he said grimly, "You would be lying in that pool yonder, by now, broken to pieces against the wheel; and I should have sought for my bird in vain." He saw how the pillow rose and fell with her breath, and how she listened.

"I wanted a bird for my Siegfried on Saturday," he went on, "Some one to sit far aloft in the flies and sing, as you sang this morning, high and pure, in the middle of the tone. Helmanoff has trained you well, child, you take the notes as if nature herself had been your teacher. Neumann is gone; she screeches like an owl! Elle a son conge!" He continued to look at the pillow and the gold curls spread across it.

"Will you come and be my bird, child? I suppose you can't act as yet; but up in the flies you will be hidden, and only your prototype will flutter across the stage on its wires. When I heard you this morning, I said to myself: 'Ha—my bird at last! Siegfried's bird!'"

He laughed softly, and bent over and stroked the curls: "I came to-night because the Neumann went off in a huff. She made a scene at rehearsal, or rather I did. I told her to go and darn stockings for a living, and she seemed to resent it!" He paused for a moment. "Saturday is only day after to-morrow—and we have no bird!"

The girl lay motionless, and the Kapellmeister went on stroking her curls. "If you sing, you will be paid, you know!" he said, "and then you need not try to kill the poor bird for lack of a crumb. Why didn't you tell me this morning, little one?"

Kaya raised her head feebly and gazed at him: "My voice is gone!" she said, "My voice is—gone!"

"Bah!" said the Kapellmeister, "With a throat like that! It is only beginning to come. The Lehmann's voice was as yours in her youth, light at first and colorature; and it grew! Mein Gott, how it grew and deepened, and swelled, and soared!— Get strong, child, and your voice will ripen like fruit in the sun."

He stooped over the pillow and looked into her eyes: "Come, child," he said, "Will you be my bird? Promise me! You won't think of that again—I can trust you? If I leave you now—"

Kaya put out her hands and clung to him suddenly, clasping his arm with her fingers. "I won't," she said, "I will live, and study, and do my best—and some day you think I shall be a singer? Oh, tell me truly! That is just what Helmanoff said, but when I asked them to hear me—I went to so many, so many!—they were always engaged, or—" She caught her breath a little, stumbling over the words: "You think so—truly?"

"I think so truly," said the Kapellmeister, "You must come to see me at the Opera-House to-morrow and rehearse your part, and I will teach you. You shall have your honorarium to-night in advance; and you must eat and grow strong."

"I will," said Kaya.

There was a new resolve in her tone, fresh hope, and she put her hand to her throat instinctively, as if to imprison the voice inside and keep it from escaping.

"Has the miller gone?" she asked.

"Yes," said Ritter, "He is gone and the door is closed; we are alone."

"Then put your head lower," whispered the girl, "and I will tell you. Perhaps, when you—know!"

"Go on," said the Kapellmeister, "I am here, child, close to you, and no one shall hurt you. Don't tremble."

"Do you see my hands?" said the girl, "Look at them. They are stained with blood—stained with—Ah, you draw away!"

"Go on," said Ritter, "You drew away yourself, child. What do you mean? What could you do with a hand like that, a rose leaf? Ha!" He laughed and clasped it with his own to give her courage: "Go on."

"You are not Russian," said the girl, "so you can't understand. When one is not Russian—to be an anarchist, to kill—that is terrible, unpardonable! But with us—My father is Mezkarpin," she whispered, "You have heard of him—yes? The great General, the friend of the Tsar! And I am the Countess Kaya, his—his daughter!"

Her voice broke, and she was silent for a moment, leaning against the pillow. Then she went on:

"There is a society," she whispered, "in St. Petersburg. It is called 'The Black Cross'; and whosoever is a member of that order must obey the will of the order; and when they pass judgment, the sentence must be fulfilled. They are just and fair. When a man, an official, has sinned only once, they pass him by; but when he has committed crime after crime, they take up his case and deliberate together, and he is judged and condemned. Sometimes it is the sentence of death, and then—" she hesitated, "and then we draw lots. The lot fell to—me."

She shut her eyes, and as the Kapellmeister watched her face, he saw that it was convulsed in agony, and the boyish look was gone.

"He was warned," she whispered, "three times he was warned, according to rule, and I—I killed him." The lines deepened in her face, and she half rose, leaning on her elbow, staring straight ahead of her as though at a vision, her lips moving:

"*In the name of the Black Cross I do now pledge myself an instrument in the service of Justice and Retribution. On whomsoever the choice of Fate shall fall, I vow the sentence of death shall be fulfilled, by mine own hands if needs be, without weakness, or hesitation, or mercy; and if by any untoward chance this hand should fall, I swear—I swear, before the third night shall have passed, to die instead—to die—instead."*

She struggled up on the bed, kneeling.

"I killed him!" she cried in a whisper, "I killed him! I see him lying on the floor there—on his face! There—there! Look! With his arms outstretched—and the blood in a pool!"

She was leaning forward over the edge of the bed, staring with her eyes dilated, pointing into the shadows and shuddering:

"Don't you see him—there?"

The Kapellmeister was white and his hands shook. He took her strongly by the shoulders. "Lie down," he said, "You are dreaming. There is nothing there. Look me in the eyes! I tell you there is nothing there, and your hands are not stained. Lie down."

Kaya gazed at him for a moment in bewilderment: "Where am I?" she said, passing her hand over her eyes. "Who are you? I thought you were—Why no, I must have been dreaming as you say."

"The hunger has made you delirious," said the Kapellmeister: "Look me in the eyes as I tell you, and I will smooth away those lines from your forehead. Sleep now—sleep!"

The girl sank reluctantly back on the pillows and the

Olive M. Briggs

Kapellmeister sat beside her, his gaze fixed on hers with a strained attention, unblinking. He was passing his hand over her forehead slowly and lightly, scarcely touching her: "Sleep—" he said, "Sleep."

Her lids wavered and drooped slowly, and she sighed and stirred against the pillows, turning on her side.

"Sleep—" he said.

The garret was still, and only the moonbeams danced on the floor. The doves in the eaves slept with their heads tucked under their wings, and the spiders were motionless in the midst of the webs; only the water was splashing below.

The Kapellmeister watched the girl on the pallet. He sat leaning back with his arms folded, his head in the shadow, and his face was grim. "She will sleep now," he said to himself, "sleep until I wake her. She is young and strong, and there is no harm done; but she has had some fearful shock, and it has shaken her like a slender birch struck by a storm. I will send my old Marta, and she will look after her—poor little bird!"

Kaya lay on her side with her face half turned to the pillow; her cheek was flushed and her breath came gently through the arch of her lips. Her curls were like a halo about her, and her right hand lay on the blanket limp, small and white with the fingers relaxed.

"I am getting to be an old man," said the Kapellmeister to himself, "and my heart is seared; but if I had a daughter, and she looked like that—I would throw over the Tsar and all his kingdom. The great Juggernaut of Autocracy has gone over her, and her wings are bruised. It is only her voice that can save her now."

He rose to his feet slowly, and in the dim light of the moon his hair was silvered, and he seemed weary and worn. He stood by the pallet, looking down at the slim, still figure for a moment; and his hand stole out and touched a strand of her hair. Then he covered her gently. "Sleep," he said, "Sleep!" And he turned and went out, closing the door.

CHAPTER XVII

"Is it only a week that I have been ill, Marta? It seems like a month."

"A week and a day, Fraeulein; but you are better now, and to-morrow, the Doctor says you shall go out on the promenade and smell of the rose buds."

Kaya was half lying, half seated on the pallet, with her hands clasped behind her head; she was dressed in a blue gown, worn and shabby but spotlessly neat, and her throat and her arms were bare. "But how soon can I sing, Marta? Did he say when? Did you hear him?"

The old nurse sat by the bed-side, knitting and counting her stitches aloud to herself from time to time.

"One—two—four—seven!" she mumbled, "Sing, Fraeulein? Ah, who can tell! You are weak yet."

"No," said Kaya, "I am strong; see my arms. I can stand up quite well and walk about the room with the help of your shoulder; you know I can, Marta."

The old woman gave her a glance over her spectacles: "Seven—ten!" she repeated, "If it were your spirit, Fraeulein, you would be Samson himself; but your body—" She shook her head: "Na, when the master comes, ask him yourself. It is he who has talked with the Doctor, not I."

"He is coming now," said Kaya. "I hear his step on the stairs, quick and firm like his beat. Don't you hear it, Marta?—Now he has stopped and is talking with the miller." She leaned back on the pillows and her eyes watched the door.

"Eh, Fraeulein! Nein, I hear nothing! What an ear you have—keen as a doe's when the wind is towards her! At home, in the forest, where the deer run wild and they come in the dawn to the Schneide to graze—whischt! The crackle of a leaf and they are off flying, with their muzzles high and their eyes wild. Na! I hear nothing but the wheel below grinding and squeaking, and the splash of the water."

"He is coming up the stairs," cried Kaya, "Open the door for him, Marta, and let the Kapellmeister in."

The old woman rolled up her knitting slowly: "It was just at the turn of the chain," she grumbled, "and I have lost a stitch in the counting. The master can come in by himself."

Kaya gave a gleeful laugh like a child, and slipped her feet to the floor: "Oh, you cross Marta, you dear humbug!" she cried, "As if you wouldn't let the master walk over you and never complain! Go on with that wonderful muffler of his, and I will let him in myself. No, don't touch me! Let me go alone and surprise him."

She steadied herself with her hand to the bed-post, then caught at the chair: "Don't touch me—Marta! I am quite strong—now, and able to—walk!"

A knock came on the door, and she made a little run forward

Olive M. Briggs

and opened it, clinging to the handle.

"Du himmlische Guete!" exclaimed the Kapellmeister, "If the bird isn't trying its wings! Behuete, child!" He put a strong arm about her, looking down at her sternly and shaking his head: "Do you call this obedience?" he said grimly, "I thought I told you not to leave that couch alone— eh?"

"Don't scold me," said Kaya, "I feel so well to-day, and there is something leaping in my throat. Herr Kapellmeister—it is begging to come out; let me try to sing, won't you?" She clung to his arm and her eyes plead with him: "Don't scold me. You have put 'Siegfried' off twice now because you had no bird. Let me try to-day."

The Kapellmeister frowned. Her form was like a lily swaying against the trunk of an oak.

"Tschut—" he said, "Bewahre! Marta, go down and bring up her soup. When your cheeks are red, child, and the shadows are gone from under your eyes, then we will see."

Kaya pushed away his arm gently, and there was a firmness about her chin as of a purpose new-born. "You have paid for my lodging and my food, Herr Kapellmeister," she said proudly, "You have sent me your own servant, and she has been to me like a foster mother. You have cared for me, and the Doctor and the medicines are all at your cost." She steadied herself, still rejecting his hand, "And I—" she said, "I have earned nothing; I have been like a beggar. If you will not let me sing, Herr Kapellmeister, then—"

He looked at her for a moment in a wounded way and his brow darkened: "Well—?" he said.

"Then you must take away your servant and the Doctor, and—and your kindness," said Kaya bravely, "and let me starve again."

"You are proud—eh? You remember that you are a Countess?" The Kapellmeister laughed harshly.

"I am not a Countess any more," said Kaya, "but I am proud. Will you let me sing?"

"When you are strong again and your voice has come back," he returned dryly, "you can sing, and not before. As for paying your debts—There is time enough for that. Now will you have the goodness to return to the couch, Fraeulein, or do you prefer to faint on the floor?"

Kaya glanced at the stern face above her, and her lip quivered: "You are angry," she said, "I have hurt you. I didn't mean to hurt you."

"The Doctor will be in presently," continued Ritter coldly, "I daresay he can restore you, if you faint, better than I. Perhaps you will obey his orders as you reject mine." There was something brutal in the tone of his voice that stung the girl like a lash. She turned and tottered back to the couch, the Kapellmeister following, his arms half extended as if to catch her if she fell; but she did not fall. He was still frowning, and he seemed moody, distraught. "Shall I cover you?" he said.

Kaya put out her hand timidly and touched his: "You have been so kind to me," she whispered, "Every day you have come, and when I was delirious I heard your voice; and Marta told me afterwards how you sat by the bed and quieted me, and put me to sleep.—Don't be angry." All of a sudden she stooped and put her lips to his sleeve.

Olive M. Briggs

He snatched his hand away roughly. "You have nothing to be grateful for," he cried, "Pah! If a man picks up a bird with a broken wing and nurses it to life again for the sake of its voice, is that cause for gratitude? I do it for my own ends, child. Tschut!" He turned his back on her and went over to the window. "If you want to know when you can sing, ask the Doctor. If he says you may—"

"You are still angry," said Kaya, "Don't be angry. If you don't want me to sing, I will lie here as you tell me and—try to get stronger." She moved her head restlessly on the pillow, "Yes—I will!"

Ritter began to strum on the window-panes with his strong fingers: "The Doctor is here," he said, "ask him. I don't want you breaking down and spoiling the opera, that is all. The rest is nothing to me. Come in!" There was a certain savageness in his tone, and he went on strumming the motive on the panes. "Come in, Doctor."

The door opened and a young man came forward. He was short of stature, and slight, with spectacles, and he stooped as if from much bending over folios.

"My patient is up?" he said.

"Walking about the room!" interrupted the Kapellmeister curtly.

The Doctor sat down by the pallet and took the girl's wrist between his fingers: "Why does it throb like this?" he said, "What is troubling you?"

"I want to sing," persisted Kaya defiantly, "If I sit in the flies with cushions behind me, and only a small, small part— couldn't I do it, Doctor?"

The young man glanced at the Kapellmeister's rugged shoulders, and shrugged his own: "Why should it hurt you?" he said, "You have a throat like a tunnel, and a sounding board like the arch of a bridge. Your voice should come tumbling through it like a stream, without effort. Don't tire yourself and let the part be short; it may do you good."

Kaya's eyes began to glisten and sparkle: "It is only the bird's part!" she cried, "and I am hidden in the flies, so no one can see me. Ah—I am happy! I am well, Doctor—you have made me well!"

Presently the old woman brought in the soup and the Doctor rose: "Will you come with me, Herr Kapellmeister?" he said, "We can smoke below in the mill, while the Fraeulein eats. I have still a few minutes."

Then the Kapellmeister left the window, and the two men went out together.

"Marta!" cried the girl, "I can sing! Did you hear him say it? Give me the soup quickly, while it is hot. I feel so strong—so well!"

She began taking the soup with one hand, and rubbing her cheek with the other: "Now, isn't it red, Marta? Look—tell me! Nurse, while you knit, tell me—did you see how angry he was, and how he went out without a word? It is he himself who asked me to sing, so why should he be angry now?"

The old woman clicked her knitting needles: "How do I know!" she said, "He lives alone so much, and he is crusty and crabbed, they say. I nursed him when he was a child, just as I nurse you now. He has a temper—Jesus-Maria—the master! But his heart is of gold. His wife—" she hesitated, "She was a singer, and she ran away and left him. They say

Olive M. Briggs

she ran away with the famous tenor, Brondi, who used to sing Tristan. Since then the master has been soured-like!"

"That is strange," said Kaya dreamily, "to run away from some one you love, when you can be with him night and day and never leave him! Sometimes there is a curse, and you are torn by your love, whether to go or stay. But if you love him enough, you go—and that is the best love—to save him from the curse and suffer yourself alone. Perhaps there was a curse."

"What are you saying?" cried the old woman, "When you were delirious, it was always a curse you raved of, and stains on your hands. Mein Gott! My blood ran cold just to hear you, and the Kapellmeister used to come—"

Kaya turned white: "He came?" she said, "and he heard me? What did I say, Marta, tell me! Tell me quickly!" She caught the old woman's hands and wrung them between her own.

"Jesus-Maria! My knitting!—What you said, Fraeulein? How do I remember! Stuff and nonsense mostly! You were crazy with fever, and your eyes used to shine so, it made me afraid. Then the Kapellmeister would come and put you to sleep with his eyes.—Let go of my hands, Fraeulein, you are crushing the wool! Is it the fever come back?—Oh Je!"

"No," said Kaya, "No. You don't remember, Marta, whether I said any name—any particular name? I didn't—did I?"

The nurse pondered for a moment, then she went on knitting: "I can't remember," she said, "There was something you used to repeat, over and over, a single word—it might have been a name. Won't you finish your soup, Fraeulein?"

"No," said Kaya, "I am tired. Will you go down, Marta, and

ask the Kapellmeister if he will come for a moment? I have something to ask him."

The nurse rose: "They are smoking still," she said, "Yes, I smell their cigars! If you have finished the soup, I will take the tray. Jesus-Maria! You are flushed, Fraeulein, and before you were so white! You are sure it is not the fever come back?"

"Feel my hands," said Kaya, "Is that fever?" Then she shut her eyes. She heard clumsy footsteps descending the stairs, and then a pause; and after a moment or two steps coming back, but they were firm and quick, and her heart kept time to them.

"What did I say in my ravings?" she cried to herself, "What did he hear?"

"Nun?" said the Kapellmeister.

"I see now what hurt you," said Kaya, without raising her eyes, "You thought I wanted to repay your kindness that can never be repaid; that I was narrow and little, and was too proud to take from your hands what you gave me. Forgive me."

The Kapellmeister crossed the room and sat down on the chair that the nurse had left. He said nothing, and Kaya felt through her closed lids that he was looking at her. "How shall I ask him?" she was saying to herself, "How shall I put it into words when perhaps he understood nothing after all?"

"If you think your voice is there," said the Kapellmeister, "fresh, and not too strained for the high notes, why you can try it now. If it goes all right, I daresay we could announce

'Siegfried' for the end of the week."

"Will you give me the note?" said Kaya, "Is it F#, or G, I forget?"

"I will hum you the preceding bars where Siegfried first hears the bird." Ritter began softly, half speaking, half singing the words in his deep voice, taking the tenor notes falsetto. "Now—on the F#. The bird must be heard far away in the branches, and you must move your head so—as it flutters from leaf to leaf."

Kaya lifted herself from the pillows until she sat upright, supporting herself with one hand. She began to sing, and then she stopped and gave a cry. "It is there!" she said pitifully, "I feel it, but it won't come!—I can't make it come! It is as if there were a gate in my throat and it was barred!"

Tears sprang to her eyes. She opened her lips farther, but the sound that came was strange and muffled; and she listened to it as if it were some changeling given to her by a mischievous demon in exchange for her own.

"That isn't my voice," she said, "You know as well as I—it never sounded like that before! What is it? Tell me—"

The Kapellmeister laughed a little, mockingly: "I told you, child," he said, "I warned you. Don't look like that! When you are stronger, it will come with a burst, and be bigger and fresher than ever before. Siegfried must wait for his bird, that is all."

Kaya clasped her throat with both hands as if to tear away the obstruction: "I will sing—I will!" she cried, "It is there—I feel it! Why won't it come out?" She gave a little moan, and threw herself back on the pillows.

The Kapellmeister stooped suddenly; a look half fierce, half pitying came in his face. He bent over her until his eyes were close to hers, and he forced her to look at him:

"What is that word you say? When you were raving, you repeated it again and again: 'Velasco—Velasco.' There is a violinist by that name, a musician."

"A—musician!" stammered Kaya. She was staring at him with eyes wide-open and frightened.

"His name is Velasco."

"Ve—las—co?"

The syllables came through her lips like a breath. "No—no!" she cried suddenly, hoarsely, "I don't know him! I—I never saw him!"

She struggled with the lie bravely, turning white to the lips and gazing. "It was some one I knew in Russia; some one I—I loved." She sat up suddenly and wrung her hands together: "You don't believe me?"

"No," said the Kapellmeister, "You can't lie with eyes like that."

Kaya gazed at him desperately: "Don't tell him," she breathed, "Ah—don't let him know—I implore you!"

Ritter gave a sharp exclamation and caught the little figure in his arms. "She has fainted!" he cried, "Potztausend, what a brute I was!" He laid her back on the pillow and stood staring down at her, breathing heavily and clenching his hands.

"If I were Velasco!" he muttered, "Ah Gott—I am mad! Marta—Marta!"

CHAPTER XVIII

The day was very warm and sultry, and the visitors, who flocked to Ehrestadt for the opera season, fanned themselves resignedly as they sat in the shaded gardens, drinking beer and liqueurs, and gossiping about the singers. The performance of 'Siegfried' was to be given that night for the second time, and they discussed it together.

"The tenor—ah, what a voice he had, and what acting, but Bruennhilde—bah!" They shook their heads. "The Schultz was growing old, and her voice was thin in the upper register; it struck against the roof of her mouth when she forced it, and sounded like tin. In the love-scene, when Bruennhilde wakes from her sleep—Tschut! What a pity a singer should ever grow old; and a still greater pity—a Jammerschade that she should go on singing!"

"The Conductor was in despair, and so were the Directors; but the contract was signed, it was too late. Ach bewahre, poor Ritter! He was in such a pique," they said, "der Arme! The bird—that was poor too, shrill and cheap! Die Neumann, who was she? Someone out of the chorus perhaps. But the Mime was splendid."

And then they went back to the great Siegfried again and praised him—"Perron! He was worth the rest of the

Olive M. Briggs

performance together, he and the orchestra; but when he had sung it with the Lehmann last year, ach—that was a different matter. He had gone through the part like a Siegfried inspired, and she—ah divine! There was no Bruennhilde to compare with her now. What a night it had been! Do you recall it?" they said—"Do you remember it?" And then the opera-goers closed their eyes ecstatically.

"The season before was better, far better!—Tschut!" And then they went on drinking their beer and liqueurs, and fanning themselves resignedly. "If the heat did not break before night-fall there would be a thunder-storm." The clouds were gathering far in the West, and the insects were humming. The air was heavy with the scent of blossoms; and the waitresses ran to and fro, dressed in Tyrolese costume; the prettier they were the more they ran.

"One beer!—Three liqueurs!" "Sogleich, meine Herren!" The garden was shady, and the glasses clinked; the tongues wagged.

"You are not afraid; you are comfortable, child, swung up there in the tree-tops?"

Kaya's eyes shone like two stars down from the green. "My heart beats," she said, "but it is only stage fright; it will pass. Is the House full?"

"Packed to the roof!"

"I am only a bird," said Kaya softly, "They won't think of me. It is Siegfried they have come to hear, and Bruennhilde. How glorious to be a Bruennhilde!"

The Kapellmeister took out his watch: "I must go," he said, "Good-bye, little one; remember what I told you, and let your voice come out without effort; not too loud, or too soft! When your part is over, one of the stage-hands will let you down again."

Kaya nodded, swinging herself childishly. "It is sweet to be a bird," she said, "I think I shall stay here always, and Siegfried will never find me."

"No—he shall never find you!" said the Kapellmeister suddenly and sharply. Their eyes met for a moment. "Are you all right?" he repeated, "You are pale."

Kaya shrank back into the leaves that were painted, and they trembled slightly as if a breeze had passed; and the great drop-curtain blew out, bulging.

"Keep the windows shut," called the voice of the stage manager, "Quick—before the curtain goes up. A storm is coming, and the draughts—oh Je!" He went hurrying past.

Ritter glanced at his watch again mechanically; then he crossed the stage to the left, and hurried down a small, winding stair-case to the pit, where the orchestra waited. A sharp tap of the baton—a glance over his men—then the second Act began.

Kaya sat very still under the leaves with the painted branches about her. She was perched on a swing, high aloft in the flies; and when she looked up, she saw nothing but ropes, and machinery, and darkness; and when she looked down, there was Mime below her, crouched by a stone; the sun was rising, the shadows were breaking, and Siegfried lay stretched at the foot of the Linden. He had long, light hair and fur about his shoulders, and he was big and splendid to look at in his youth and his wrath. He was threatening Mime, and the dwarf was muttering and cursing. Beyond was the pit

Olive M. Briggs

with the orchestra, the footlights, the House.

Kaya listened, and her thoughts went back to St. Petersburg and the class of Helmanoff. She was singing to him, and when she had finished, he had taken her hands. "If you were not a Countess," he said, "you could be a Lehmann in time, another Lehmann." Kaya leaned her curls against the rope of the swing dreamily. "How long ago that seems," she said to herself, "before—before I—"

Then she thought of the weeks since her illness, and how her voice had come back suddenly, over night as it were, only bigger and fuller; and how she had worked and studied, day after day, rehearsing with Ritter.

Her brow clouded a little as she remembered. He had been severe, the Kapellmeister, caustic, even irritable. How hard he was to satisfy! When she sang her best, he shrugged his shoulders; when she sang badly, he was furious. Occasionally he was kind as to-day, but not often. . . . Siegfried was alone now, carving his reed, trying to mimic the song of the wood birds. . . . The Kapellmeister had said nothing of Lehmann; perhaps she had lost her voice after all. Her thoughts rambled on as she waited for her cue. . . .

Siegfried's horn was to his lips and he was blowing it; a splendid figure, eager, expectant. . . . Kaya stretched her throat like a bird: "If it should be barred," she said to herself, "as it was before, and the orchestra began with the theme, and I couldn't sing!" She trembled a little.

So the first scene passed; and the second.

The Dragon was on the stage now, and Siegfried was fighting him. The hot breath poured from the great, red nostrils; the sword flashed. The battle grew fiercer. . . . Kaya leaned over, stooping in the swing, and gazing. "Siegfried has wounded him," she whispered,—"in a moment the sword will have reached his heart. . . . Ah, now—it has struck him—he is dying! As soon as he is dead! As soon as he is— dead."

The orchestra was playing passionately, and she knew every note; the bird motive came nearer and nearer. Already her prototype was being prepared in the flies, and the wires made ready. She clung to the rope, swinging. . . . Ah, how good the Kapellmeister had been to her; how good! It was his very interest in her that had made him severe, she knew that. She must sing her best, and not wound him by failure.

The motive came nearer.

Siegfried was standing just below her now. She took a deep breath and her lips parted. He was peering up at her, searching through the leaves, and the bird on its wire fluttered across the stage. . . . She was singing. The notes, high and pure, poured out of her throat. The bird fluttered past.

She swayed, with her head leaning back against the ropes, and sang—and sang. Her throat was like a tunnel and her voice was like a stream running through it, clear and glorious. Siegfried looked up and started. The orchestra played on.

"Has the Fraeulein gone home?"

"No," said Marta, yawning, "She is in one of the dressing-rooms. I begged her to come, but she wouldn't."

The Kapellmeister laid his hand on her shoulder carelessly: "If you are sleepy," he said, "go back to the mill; I will bring

Olive M. Briggs

her myself presently. The House is dark now, and the people are going." He gave a curt nod, dismissing the old woman, and strode on through the wings.

One person after another stopped him: "Ha, Kapellmeister, where did that nightingale hail from?"

"I snared it for you, Siegfried; were you satisfied?"

"Ach, mein Gott! I thought I was back on the Riviera, and it was moon-light.—Snare me another Bruennhilde, can't you?" The great tenor laughed and put his finger to his lips: "Singing with the Lehmann spoils one," he said, "Bah—! It was frightful to-night! She grows always worse. Would the bird were a goddess instead." He waved his hand: "Good-night!"

"Good-night," said the Kapellmeister, hurrying on.

"Ritter—hey! Stop a moment! What has come over the Neumann?"

"Nothing, Jacobs—nothing! She is dead."

Mime straightened his back that was stiff from much crouching: "Ausgeworfen?"

"Ja wohl."

"Then who is the lark?"

"An improvement you think—eh?"

The singer laughed: "The way Perron jumped! Did you see him? With the first note he gaped open-mouthed into the branches, and came within an ace of dropping his sword. I chuckled aloud in the wings. Who is she, Kapellmeister?"

"Good-night—good-night!" cried Ritter, "excuse me, but I am late and in a hurry. This opera conducting is frightfully wearing; I am limp as a rag. Good-night!" he ran on.

The doors of the dressing-rooms stood open, and he peered into them, one after the other. In some the electric light was still on, and the costumes were scattered about on the open trunks. The principals were gone already, and most of the chorus; and the men of the orchestra went hurrying by like shadows, with their instruments under their arms. In the House itself, behind the asbestos curtain, which was lowering slowly, came the sound of seats swinging back, and the voices of the ushers as they rushed to and fro.

"Kaya!" called the Kapellmeister softly, "Where are you?" He hurried from room to room.

The dressing-room of Madame Schultz was on the second floor, up a short, winding stair-case, and the lights were turned low. Ritter paused in the doorway.

The prima-donna was standing before the pier-glass, still in costume; her soft, white robes trailed over the floor, and her red-blonde hair hung to her waist. The helmet glittered on her head, and she held her spear aloft as if about to utter the Walkuere cry. The figure was superb, magnificent; a goddess at bay. And as the Kapellmeister stared at her in astonishment, he saw that she was tense with emotion.

"Madame," he stammered, "You! You—still here?"

Her face was to the glass, her back to the door; she wheeled about quickly and faced him: "Yes, I am here!" she cried, "Bruennhilde is here! The House was cold to me to-night—

they clapped Perron. It was all Siegfried. They would have hissed me if they had dared." The spear shook in her trembling hand.

"When my voice broke in the top notes, you could hear them whispering in the loggias; didn't you hear them? 'She is old,' they said, 'she can't sing any more, or act! She has no business to be here. Get us another Bruennhilde!' And the stage hands looked at me pityingly. I saw! Do you think I am blind and deaf as well as old? Look at me as I stand here! I am Bruennhilde!"

The form of the singer was rigid, drawn to its height; the head thrown back and the helmet glittering on her red-blonde hair. Her eyes were proud and scornful.

"Am I not—Bruennhilde?"

"Yes—yes!" cried Ritter, drawing back in a dazed way: "You are magnificent, Madame. If you had acted like that tonight, you would have had the House at your feet."

The singer took a step forward. "It is not I," she cried, "It is Bruennhilde herself! Come, let her sing to you! The scene is still there on the stage, the rocks and the fir-tree—and Bruennhilde's couch. The fire motive seethes in my brain, and the flames are springing. Come—and waken me!"

She grasped his sleeve with her fingers, and drew him: "You are not the Kapellmeister!" she cried, "You are Siegfried, and you must sing the part in falsetto. Come!"

Ritter gave a quick glance about. The stage hands were gone, and the singers. The stage was in semi-darkness, half lighted, and the scene was unchanged. He could see it from the top of the balustrade. There was no one in the House behind, or in front, and the foot-lights were out; only the porter watched below, half asleep and waiting. He was alone with a mad woman; Bruennhilde gone crazy and frantic with grief because she was old and her voice was gone. She was dragging at his hand, and pulling him towards the stair-case. He followed her dumbly.

"Come—come!" she panted, "You think the Schultz has gone mad! No—no! It is only her youth come back, and her voice is leaping in her throat. She must sing—must sing! There is the couch. See, I fling myself on it! I am covered with the shield, and the spear lies beside me. You have wakened me, Siegfried, with your kiss; and now I raise myself slowly. I am dazed—I stare blindly about! Hark, how the fire is leaping and crackling!"

The singer was seated upright now on the couch, and Ritter was standing helpless beside her. As she acted, the blood ran cold in his veins. It was true what she had said. She was no longer the Schultz: she was Bruennhilde herself, the goddess, and the kiss of Siegfried was on her lips.

She was singing now; she had sprung to her feet with the spear in her hand, and the music poured from her throat. It was not the voice of Schultz; it was richer and fuller, and the tones were deep and strong, and pure and high; and it rang out and filled the empty stage like a clarion trumpet, silver-toned. She held her hands high above her head, waving the spear; coming nearer to him and nearer.

"O Siegfried, Herrliche Hort der Welt!
Leben der Erde, lachender Held!"

Her red-blonde hair shone in the light and the helmet glittered: "Siegfried! Siegfried!"

It was the Lehmann come back! Ah, no—it was more than the Lehmann! Ritter gazed and listened, and his heart gave a leap. It was Bruennhilde herself, the goddess come to life; and the stage was no longer there: it was night on the mountain-top; they were surrounded by fires crackling and leaping; the flash of flames curling, and light and smoke. The violins were playing.

Instinctively his fingers clutched the air as if grasping the baton. "Siegfried!"

The cry came big and passionate as from the throat of a Walkuere, without limit or strain. The Kapellmeister staggered and covered his eyes.

"Gott!" he cried, "Am I dreaming? Where am I? Madame— stop! Are you the Schultz, or are you—? I thought you were mad, stark mad; but it is I—I! When I looked at you now, you were Bruennhilde alive—your voice is the voice of the goddess herself!"

He sank down on the couch and covered his face with his hands. The blood rushed to his ears and seethed there, and the music beat against his brain. Then the faintness passed, and he looked up.

Bruennhilde stood a little apart, still grasping the spear. The light fell on her helmet, and it shone; her lips were arched as if the tones were still in her throat, dying away. She was gazing at him and her breast was panting. The light fell full on her face.

"Ach—mein Gott!" he cried, "It is Kaya!"

CHAPTER XIX

"Yes, it is I," said Kaya.

She put up both hands, lifting the helmet from her head, and the red-blonde hair fell back from her short, gold curls. The spear dropped with a clang to the stage and lay extended between them, glittering.

"My voice was there," she said softly, "in my throat, leaping and bounding, and the gate was unbarred." She seemed half afraid, and drew back in the shadow.

Ritter still sat on the edge of the couch, where Bruennhilde had lain, and where Siegfried had kissed her. His face had a dazed look, and he passed his hand over his eyes several times, as if the dusk were too dim for his sight.

"I thought you were the Schultz gone mad!" he murmured. "Gott! What an actress you are!"

A laugh came to him out of the darkness.

"You are no bird," said Ritter, "You are a Walkuere born. Take the helmet again and the spear. As you stood in the shadow, gazing downward, you were like a young warrior watching his shield." He sprang to his feet and came toward

Olive M. Briggs

her, placing the spear in her hand, the helmet again on her head.

"Sing," he said, "Let me hear it again. Your voice is a marvel! The timbre is silver and the tones are of bronze. Let me look at your throat! Gott—but the roof of your mouth is arched like a dome and the passage is as the nave of a cathedral, wide and deep!"

His hand grasped her shoulder, trembling: "Did Helmanoff know you had a voice like that?" he cried, "Tell me, child, did he train you? The part is most difficult to act and to sing. Tell me—or am I dreaming still?"

Kaya fingered the spear dreamily: "My voice is bigger and fuller," she said; "it came so all of a sudden, but he taught me the part, and he told me, some day, if I were not a Countess I could become the Bruennhilde." Her form stiffened suddenly and she threw off his grasp, springing forward and crouching:

"You are Wotan and you are angry," she whispered, "The Bruennhilde is your child and she has sinned. You have threatened her, and now she is pleading: 'Wotan—Father!'" Her voice rose, and her form shook as though with sobs. She crept closer, still crouching, and lay at his feet, and her voice was like something crying and wrestling.

"Hier bin ich Vater: Gebiete die Strafe . . .
Du verstoesest mich? Versteh' ich den Sinn?
Nimmst du mir alles was einst du gabst?"

Her voice sobbed, dying away into a tone pure, soft, heart-breaking, like a breath; yet it penetrated and filled the stage, the wings, and came echoing back.

"Hier bin ich Vater; Gebiete die Strafe . . .
Du verstoesest mich?"

For a moment she lay as if exhausted; then she covered her head with her hands as if fearing and trembling: "Now curse me," she whispered, "Curse me! I hear the flames now beginning to crackle!"

The Kapellmeister put out his hand and took hers, and lifted her: "If the House were full," he said, "and you acted like that, they would go stark mad; they would shower bouquets at your feet and carry you on their shoulders. The Lehmann was the great Bruennhilde, but you are greater, Kaya. Your voice has the gift of tears. When you let it out, one is thrilled and shaken, and there is no end to the glory and power; it encircles one as with a wreath of tones. But when you lower it suddenly and breathe out the sound—child—little one, what have you suffered to sing like that? You are young. What must you have suffered!"

He clasped her hands tenderly between his own, and stared down into her eyes.

"Don't touch me," she said brokenly, "I told you—there is blood on them! I am cursed like Bruennhilde. The curse is in my voice and you hear it, and it is that that makes you tremble and shudder—just as I tremble and shudder—at night—when I dream, and I see the body beside me on the floor—and the red pool—widening. Helmanoff used to tell me my voice was cold and pure like snow; there was no feeling, no warmth, no abandon. You see—if I have learned it, it is not Helmanoff who has taught me—but suffering."

Her eyes were like two fires burning, and she put her hand to her throat. "To have the gift of tears you must have shed them," she whispered, looking at him strangely: "You must have—shed them."

"Is it the curse alone," said the Kapellmeister, "that keeps you and Velasco apart, little one? Forgive me! Don't start like that! Don't—don't tremble."

Kaya backed away from him, snatching away her hands. Her lips were quivering and her eyes half closed. "Ah—" she breathed, "You are cruel. Take the spear and strike me, but don't prod a wound that is open and will not—heal! Have you no wound of your own hidden that you must needs bare mine?"

"It is love that has taught you," said the Kapellmeister, "You love him—Velasco!"

She gave a low moan and flung her arms up, covering her face.

The Kapellmeister stared at her for a moment. The stage was dark, and only a bulb of light, here and there, gleamed in the distance. Below, the watchman was pacing the corridor, waiting, and the smell of his pipe came up through the wings. The scenery looked grim and ghostly; the couch of Bruennhilde lay bare. Above were ropes and machinery dangling, and darkness.

He clinched his teeth suddenly and a sound escaped him, half a cry, half a groan; but smothered, as though seized and choked back. "Come," he said. He went to her roughly and took the helmet from her head, and the shield, and the spear; she standing there heedless with her arms across her face. They fell to the floor with a crash, first one, then the other, and the sound was like a blow, repeating itself in loud echoes.

"Go and take off your things," he said hurriedly, "It is midnight—past, and the watchman is waiting to lock the stage door. Rouse yourself—go! I will wait for you here."

He heard the sound of her footsteps crossing the stage, ascending the stair-case; and he walked backwards and forwards, forwards and backwards, in and out among the rocks and the trees. His forehead was scarred with lines, and his shoulders were bent. The look of the victorious General about him had changed into the look of one who has met the enemy face to face, and has fought with his strength and his might, and been beaten, with his forces slain and a bullet in his breast.

His eyes were fierce and his face set, his feet stumbled; he was white as death and weary. He heard her coming back and he walked on, backwards and forwards, without looking or heeding.

"Have you your cloak?"

"Yes."

"An umbrella?"

"No."

"It is raining. Don't you hear it, and the thunder in the distance? The storm has broken. Come, we will take a cab." He strode across the stage and down the staircase; she following. He nodded to the watchman:

"Still rehearsing," he said shortly, "Sorry to keep you up. Whistle, will you, for a Droschke? Gott! The rain is terrific; hear it! Come."

There was the sound of wheels, of horses' hoofs.

He went forward and opened the door of the Droschke, and Kaya crept in.

She was no longer the Bruennhilde; she was a little figure, slight and pale, and wrapped in a cloak; and she sat in the corner against the cushions, staring out at the rain, quivering at the thunder crashes.

Ritter stepped in behind her and closed the door. "Nonnen-Muehle!" he cried, "and drive fast. We are chilled to the bone! The storm grows worse; it is devilish late!" He flung himself back in the opposite corner, and the Droschke rolled on.

It was still in the carriage. From outside came the sound of the rain falling, and the hoofs of the horses trotting. Kaya shut her eyes. The rhythmical sound caught her senses. She was in St. Petersburg again, and driving in the darkness through the night and the storm; and Velasco was beside her—Velasco! They were driving to the church to be— married.

"Don't do that again," cried the Kapellmeister fiercely, "I can't bear it."

"W—what?"

"You moaned."

Kaya crept closer into the corner, and clasped the cloak to her breast and throat.

"It is like seeing a bird with a shot in its breast—in torture," he said, "And when you sing, it is like a swan song. Your soul is on your lips, crying out, imploring.—Kaya!"

He bent over the shrinking form in the corner: "I was brutal to you; my heart was sore, seeing you suffer. The words came out like a lash; they cut you. I saw how they hurt you. Little one—if I bare the wound to the air again, forgive me— forgive me! No—don't shrink away. If you love him like that, my God—I know him! He comes to my house! Only a few weeks ago he was there, and he's coming again; soon, I tell you, soon. I swear I will bring him to you! If he won't come, I will force him; with my hands I will drag him if he refuses."

The girl gave a cry: "Drag him!" she cried, "Force him! Ah, he'd fly at a word—he'd fly to me!" She caught her breath: "Bozhe moi!" she said suddenly, and laughed: "What are you talking about, dear Master? Velasco—he's nothing to me! A musician, you said—a violinist! You forget I am Bruennhilde to-night. We talked of a curse—not love. Siegfried is still behind the flames and cannot get past."

She laughed again, a sound like a trill: "You forget, don't you?" she said, "I was acting a part! It wasn't real; I was only playing—pretending. How the Schultz cheated you! Ah, dear Master—you thought she had lost her wits and her size all at once. You never noticed how she had shrunken; and that was because I stood on tip-toe, and held myself straight with the helmet. If the light hadn't fallen full on my face, you would never have guessed! I laughed to myself; how I laughed! I— laughed!"

"Child," said the Kapellmeister suddenly. "You are sobbing!"

"I am not—I am laughing, dear Master. Look at me! There is the mill across the promenade. How gaunt the wheel looks, and strange, with its spokes dripping, and the rain lashing down! And there is a light in my window—a candle, see? Old Marta is waiting, and how she will scold. Tell me, Master—dear Master, before we get there, tell me—some day may I act Bruennhilde and sing, when the curtain is up, and the House is full, and Siegfried is there, and you at the baton—and the orchestra playing? Tell me!"

She drew closer to him, and the last words came out in a whisper, breathless and eager. "Put those other thoughts out of your mind, dear Kapellmeister. Ve—Velasco is only a name—nothing more!

"If I can sing I will be happy; I promise you. The sting of the curse will—pass. You are silent and cold!" she cried, "You won't tell me, and we are almost there—at the mill! Master!"

The Kapellmeister started: "The mill?" he stammered, "What were you saying, Kaya? How cold your hand is, little one! Of course you shall sing. You shall be our great Bruennhilde and the visitors will flock to Ehrestadt, and you will be famous and beloved."

He hesitated: "I can't see you, only your eyes gleaming, Kaya. How bright they are, little one, like live coals! Where did you get that name—'Master'? Did Marta teach you? My pupils say that, the chorus, the orchestra, and the singers; but you never used it before. It is because I am old now and my hair is grey, and you are a child. I must seem to you like your father, Kaya."

"No," said the girl quickly, "not my father! He was hard and cruel; he was a friend of the Tsar. I—I never loved him."

"Nor me," cried the Kapellmeister hoarsely, "Nor me!"

The words sprang to his lips in spite of himself; they were low, and he thought she did not hear; but her ear was keen. She bent forward taking his hand, and kissed it swiftly, holding it between her own.

"Dear Kapellmeister! Dear Master!" she cried, half laughing, half with a sob: "You know I love you. When I was ill and alone, and desperate, and helpless, longing to die, you came to me. You saved me and helped me; and I was nothing to you but a stranger. You were father and mother to me; and now, you are my master, and teacher, and friend." She lifted his hand again to her lips and caressed it: "I love you," she cried, "dear Master, I love you with all my heart!"

Ritter stirred against the cushions; his hand lay limp in her clasp. "Yes, little one," he said, "Yes. Your heart is like your voice, fathomless and pure. The carriage has stopped now, and there is the candle, burning up yonder under the eaves. Can you find your way alone, without help? I am strangely weary."

His voice was low, and the words came slowly, with an effort. He passed his hand over his face:

"Good-night—Bruennhild'!"

He held her hands and drew her towards him: "Good-night, little one. There are shadows under your eyes, and your lip quivers; you are pale.—Good-night." He held her for a moment in a strong grasp, staring down into her face; then she was gone and the door closed behind her. His hands were empty, and the horses had turned, and were galloping back through the rain and the night.

Olive M. Briggs

CHAPTER XX

It was dusk, and the lights of the Rathskeller began to twinkle out one by one. The Keller was long and rambling, divided into innumerable small alcoves and corners, partitioned by strange and antique carvings.

The ceiling was low, with octagonal vaults like a cloister. On the smoke-grimed walls, here and there, were mural paintings of knights in armour, and fat peasants drinking, dimmed and half obliterated. Beneath were legends and proverbs, printed in quaint, old-German characters; while across one end, like a frieze, ran a ledge carven with gargoyles, rude and misshapen. On the ledge were beer mugs of every size and description, with queer tops and crooked handles. Above, suspended from the ceiling by chains, hung a huge Fass; and from the throats of the gargoyles, dragon and devil alike, dripped the beer, turned on by small taps hidden.

In and out, among the tables, sped the waitresses in their Tyrolese costume with its picturesque head-dress; and beyond lay the garden, innumerable bulbs of light gleaming like fire-flies among the trees.

"Bitte um zwei Muenchener!"

"Sogleich, meine Herren."

"Ein Chartreuse und ein Pilsener!"

"Jawohl! Sofort!"

And the waitresses sped, vying with one another, coquetting with their patrons, smiling gayly with sharp retorts; their eyes bright, their trays laden with foaming beer mugs.

In one of the alcoves, far back in the shadow, sat two gentlemen. The younger had removed his hat, and was pushing the hair impatiently back from his brows. His eyes were dark and sleepy, half covered by the brows, weighed down by the lids.

He was leaning on one elbow and responded languidly to his companion, half heeding, toying with his hands, and strumming on the table with his fingers, which were white, and supple, and full of magnetism.

Beside him lay a violin.

"You are nervous to-night, Velasco?"

"I am always nervous."

"What shall we eat and drink?"

"Donnerwetter—what you please! If I eat, I cannot play. Bring me some of that Rhine wine, Fraeulein, the white in the slanting bottles, and a plate of Pretzeln. No beer— bewahre!"

The Musician raised his hands with a shrug of his shoulders, and then sank back in his former listless attitude.

"That is your Polish taste, Velasco. Try a bit of Schinken with me, or a Stueckchen of Cervelat with cheese—eh? If you eat, you will be less nervous, and your fingers will become warm. When you play, you are abstinent as a priest before the mass."

The older man smoothed his beard, which was fast turning grey, and lifted the beer mug to his lips.

"Ich danke!" said Velasco with irony: "My dear Kapellmeister, I am not as those who would serve Art with a bottle of champagne under each arm. I want no fumes in my brain and no clod between my fingers when I meet the Muse face to face."

"You are right there," said Ritter thoughtfully, lowering his glass: "It is like a pearl coming out of the throat of a swine to hear the tones from Bauermann's fingers, when he can scarce keep himself at the pianoforte, and his head rocks between his shoulders like a top falling. His sense of beauty is all that is left of him, and that seems over ripe, like a fruit left too long in the sun. Materialism is the artist's curse. Their heads are in the clouds and their feet are in the slough.—Pah!"

The Kapellmeister tapped his glass sharply with the edge of his knife, and called without turning: "Hey—a Muenchener, Fraeulein!"

He scanned the face of his companion curiously. The Violinist seemed to be dreaming; he held the Rhine wine in his hand, gazing down into its liquid gold as if a vision lay at the bottom of the glass.

"Velasco!"

The Musician half raised his lids and then lowered

them again.

"Are you asleep, Velasco?"

"Potztausend—no! I hear what you say! You speak of musicians and swine in the same breath. It is true. You ought to know, who wave the baton over them year in and year out. They rise like a balloon and then they fall—!"

He dropped his hands on the table with an expressive gesture. "They give out through the senses; they take in the same way." He lifted the glass, staring into it again: "But it is not through pleasure, not pleasure, Ritter, never pleasure, that their senses are developed, and they learn to feel, and give back what they have felt. They think it is pleasure, and they fall into the error, and their art dies within them sooner or later. It is like some fell thing clutching at their feet, and when they try to rise, it seizes them and drags them back, and they sink finally—they sink!"

The Kapellmeister leaned forward on the table, scanning the young face opposite him: "A year ago, Velasco, your chin was round and full; from the look of your mouth one could tell that you had lived and enjoyed. You were like the Faun, happy and careless, and your art was to you like a plaything. You cared only for your Stradivarius, and when you were not playing, you were nothing, not even a man. All your genius was concentrated there in your brows where the music lies hidden. Your virility was in your tones, and your strength in your fingers. What has come over you?"

"Am I changed?" said Velasco. His throat contracted. He held the glass to his lips, but he did not drink.

The Kapellmeister gazed at him strangely: "Yes, you are changed. In one year you have grown ten. What it is I cannot tell, but the look of your face is different. The mouth has grown rugged and harsh; there are lines under your eyes, and your lips are firm, not full. It is as if a storm had burst on a young birch, and torn it from its bank amid the grass and the heather, and an oak had grown up in its place, brought into life by the wind and the gale."

Velasco tossed off the Moselle and laughed bitterly: "I have done with pleasure," he said, "I have lived and I know life; that is all. There is nothing in it but work and music."

"Tell me, Velasco," said the Kapellmeister slowly, "Don't be offended if I ask, or think that I am trying to pry into your affairs. When you were rehearsing this morning it occurred to me.—There was something new in the quality of your tone. Before, you were a virtuoso; your technique was something to gaze at and harken to, and there was no technique like it in Europe; now—"

"Well—now?" cried Velasco, "Was I clumsy this morning? Was anything the matter? Potztausend!—why didn't you tell me?"

His eyes gleamed suddenly under his brows and he twirled his fingers, toying with them nervously. "Gott— Kapellmeister! Why didn't you tell me at once?"

"Now—" said the Kapellmeister: He looked up at the Bierfass, hanging by its chains, and his gaze wandered slowly over the legends on the wall, the gargoyles dripping; the mugs with their quaint tops and their handles twisted, the roof in its octagonal vaults, smoky, begrimed; and then back again to the table, and the flask before Velasco, yellow and slanting.

"Now—" he said, "you are no longer a virtuoso, you are an

artist, and that, as you know, is something infinitely greater and higher and more difficult of attainment. All the great violins of my time I have heard; most of them I have conducted."

Ritter's voice lowered suddenly to a whisper, and he leaned forward, touching the other's hand with his own: "I tell you, Velasco, and I know what I say—you played to-day at rehearsal as none of them played, not even Sarasati, king of virtuosi; or Joachim, prince of artists. You played as if the violin were yourself, and your bow were tearing your own heart strings. . . . Don't move! Don't get up! What is it, Velasco? You are white as death and your eyes are staring! Listen to my question and answer it, or not, as you please. This is not an age of miracles. The birch was not torn from the bank without reason, or the oak transplanted. Tell me— have you ever loved a woman?"

There was a sudden silence in the Rathskeller. It was almost deserted, and the waitresses were all in the garden, running forward and backward under the trees. From outside came the sound of voices and glasses clinking; and close by, from the ledge, the slow trickle of the beer through the throats of the gargoyles.

"Look at them!" said Velasco dreamily: "It is the Pilsener that runs through the dragons' mouths, and the Muenchener through the devils'; a bizarre fancy that!"

He stooped and struck a match against the table edge, lighting his cigarette. "These are Russian, Kapellmeister, extra brand! Try one! I prefer them to Turkish myself." He leaned his head against the carvings of the partition, and drew the smoke in through his nostrils slowly, his eyes half closed.

"It is a quarter to eight now," said Ritter, "but there is plenty of time.—I shouldn't have asked that question perhaps, Velasco. Forgive me. My own affairs have turned my thoughts too much on that subject."

"Was it several years ago?" said Velasco, "I don't remember." He passed his hand over his forehead several times as if chafing his memory.

Ritter pushed away his plate, and leaned forward with his head on his hands, staring down at the table, and tracing out the pattern of the wood with his fingers.

"Fourteen years to-night, Velasco. I have never spoken of it to any one; but somehow to-night it would be a relief to talk. Brondi was staying at my house; he was the Tristan. One night he gave out he was ill, and some one else took the part. When I returned from the opera, he was gone and she was gone, and the house was dark and deserted."

Ritter was silent for a moment.

"Fourteen years to-night, Velasco, and I feel as if it were yesterday."

The Violinist shaded his eyes from the light as if it hurt him: "When you came back," he said, "When you found out— what was it you felt, love or hate?"

The Kapellmeister made a swift, repelling gesture as if some reptile had touched him: "Love!" he cried, "Hate! Velasco— man, there is many a sin at my door; I am far from a saint heaven knows; but to deceive one who has trusted—to desert one who has loved and been loyal! God! There is no worse crime than that, or more despicable! Can one love, or hate, where there is only contempt?"

He clenched his fist, and his eyes were like two sword points boring into the face opposite.

"Contempt—" he said, "It has eaten into my heart like a poisonous drug and killed all else. There is nothing left."

The Kapellmeister took a long breath, then he continued hoarsely: "But I am a man; with a woman it is different. Her heart is young and she knows nothing of the world. It is like a stab in the dark from a hand she loves, and her heart is torn. If she is brave, facing the world with a smile on her lips, she bleeds inwardly. She is like a swan, swooping in circles lower and lower, with a song in her throat, until the great wings droop, and the eyes grow dim, and she falls finally, and the song is stilled. But the last beat of her heart and the last echo of her voice is for him—for him who fired the shot in her breast!"

He half rose in his seat with his hands trembling, and then sank back again.

"Have you ever loved a woman and left her, Velasco? Tell me—have you a deed like that on your conscience?"

"I—?" The Musician laughed aloud and took his hand from his face: "You are talking in riddles, Kapellmeister! The beer has gone to your head, and you are drunk! Look at the clock over yonder!—What is love? A will-o'-the-wisp! You chase it and it eludes you; you clasp it and it melts into air! There is nothing in life, I tell you, but music and work."

He poured out another glass of the wine: "Here's to your health, Kapellmeister! Prosit—my friend! Put those grim thoughts from your mind, and women from your heart. We must be off."

He was quaffing the liquor at a gulp.

"Prosit, Kapellmeister!"

Ritter made no answer. He sat staring moodily down at the table. "You are young, Velasco, to be bitter. Is it music, or work, that has carven those lines in your face?"

There was a sting in his voice.

The Violinist threw back his head like a horse at the touch of the spur. His eyes blazed defiantly at the Kapellmeister for a moment, and then the light went out of them as flame from a coal. The glass fell from his hand and lay shattered in fragments on the floor. He stood looking down at them wearily:

"That is my life," he said, "It is broken like the glass; and the wine is my love. There is nothing left of it but a stain. It has gone from me and is dead. Come!"

He lifted his violin, and the two men took their hats and went out, side by side, silently, without speaking.

The room was empty. Slowly from the throats of the gargoyles trickled the beer; and the Fass was like a great shadow hung from the ceiling by its chains. From outside came the clamour of voices and laughter, and the waitresses sped to and fro. The lights twinkled gayly under spreading of the leaves, and the glasses clinked.

CHAPTER XXI

The Friedrichs-Halle was old and shabby and had originally been a market. The entrance was under an arcade, and there was an underground passage, connecting the green-room with the stage-door of the Opera House; a passage narrow and ill-smelling, without windows or light; but dear to the hearts of musicians by reason of its associations.

Mendelssohn had walked there, and Schumann, and Brahms; and the air, as it could not be changed, was the same. The very microbes were musical, and the walls were smudged with snatches of motives, jotted down for remembrance.

"Is there a seat left in the top gallery—just one?"

"Standing room only, Madame."

The ticket-seller, who sat in a box-like room under the arcade, handed out a slip of green paste-board, and then shut the window with a slam. The gesture of his hand expressed the fact that his business was now over. Standing room also had ceased, and the long line of people waiting turned away with muttered exclamations.

The foyer was like an ant-hill in commotion; people running forwards and backwards, trying vainly to bribe an entrance, until the noise was like hornets buzzing; while from behind came the sound of the orchestra tuning, faint raspings of the cellos, and the wails of the wood-winds, and above them the cry of a trumpet muffled.

Kaya took the green paste-board hastily in her hand, clasping it, as if afraid it might in some way be snatched from her, and sped up the narrow stone stairway to the right, running fast until her breath failed her. Still another turn, and another flight, and she stood in the Concert Hall, high up under the roof, where the students go, and the air is warm and heavy, and the stage looks far away. The gallery was crowded.

On the stage the orchestra were assembling, still tuning occasionally here and there where an instrument was refractory. The scores lay open and ready on the desks. A hum of excitement was over the House, and one name was on every lip: "Velasco!"—the Polish violinist, the virtuoso, the artist, whose fame had spread over all Europe.

In Berlin he had had a furore; in Dresden the orchestra had carried him on their shoulders, shouting and hurrahing; in Leipzig, even Leipzig, where the critics are cold, and they have been fed music from their cradles, the glory of him had taken them all by storm.

"Velasco!"

The orchestra stood quietly now, expectant, each behind his desk. A hush crept over the House. The people leaned forward watching. It was past the hour.

Kaya stood wrapped in her cloak, leaning against the wall. Her head was bare, and her hair was like a boy's, curling in rings and shining in the light. Her eyes were fixed on the little door at the end of the stage. Every time it opened slightly she started, and her heart gave a throb. The air grew heavier.

When it finally opened, it was Ritter who came out. He strode hastily across the Stage, nodding shortly as if aware that the ripple of applause was not for him; then he took his place on the Conductor's stand with his back to the House, and waited, the baton between his fingers. The door opened again.

Kaya covered her eyes for a moment, and a little thrill went through her veins. She swayed and leaned heavily against the wall.

God! It was seven months and a day since that night in the inn. She was in his arms again, and he was bending over her, whispering hoarsely, his voice full of repressed anger and emotion:

"Lie still, Kaya, lie still in my arms! The gods only know why you said it, but it isn't the truth! You love me—say you love me; say it, Kaya! Let me hear you, my beloved!"

He was pressing his lips to hers.

"Take away your lips—Velasco!"

Then she recovered herself with a start, and took her hand from her eyes.

The door was ajar. Velasco was coming through it carelessly, gracefully, with his violin under his arm; and as he came, he bowed with a half smile on his lips, tossing his hair from his brow.

The audience was nothing to him; they were mere puppets,

and as they shouted and clapped, welcoming him with their lips and their hands, he bowed again, slightly, indifferently, and laid the Stradivarius to his shoulder, caressing the bow with his fingers.

Ritter struck the desk sharply with his baton and the orchestra began to play, drowning the applause; and it ceased gradually, dying away into silence.

Then Velasco raised his bow.

There was a hush, a stillness in the air, and he drew it over the strings—one tone, deep and pure with a rainbow of colours, shading from fortissimo, filling the House, to the faintest piano—pianissimo, delicate, elusive; breathing it out, and pressing on the string with his finger until it penetrated the air like an echo, and the bow was still drawing slowly, quiveringly.

He swayed as he played, laying his cheek to the violin; the waves of dark hair falling over his brows. His fingers danced over the strings, and his bow began to leap and sparkle. The audience listened spellbound, without a whisper or move-ment. The orchestra accompanied, but the sound of the violins in unison was as nothing to the single cry of the Stradivarius.

It sang and soared, it was deep and soft; it was like the sighing of the wind through the forest, and the tones were like a voice. From his instrument, his bow, his fingers, himself, went out a strange, mesmeric influence that seemed to stretch over the House, the audience, bending it, forcing it to his will; compelling it to his mood.

As he played on and on, the influence grew stronger, more pervading, until his personality was as a giant and the audience pigmies at his feet, sobbing as his Stradivarius sobbed; laughing when it laughed; crying out with joy, or with pain, with frenzy or delight, as his bow rent the strings. He scarcely heeded them. His eyes were closed and he rocked the violin in his arms, swaying as in a trance.

Kaya crouched against the wall; and as she listened, she gazed until it seemed as if her eyes were blinded, and she could no longer make out the slim lines of his figure, the dark head, and the bow leaping.

The tones struck against her brain with a thrill of concussion like hail against a roof. It was as if he were calling to her, pleading with her, embracing her.

She stretched out her arms to him and the tears ran down her face. "Velasco!" she murmured, "Velasco—come back! Put your arms around me! Don't look at me like that! I love you—come back!"

But no sound left her throat, and the cloak pinioned her arms. She was crouching against the wall, and gazing and trembling: "Velasco—!"

How different he was! When he had played at the Mariinski, and she had tossed the violets from her loggia, he was a boy, a virtuoso. Life and fame were before him; and he sprang out on the stage like a young Apollo, eager and daring. And now—She searched his face.

There were lines there; shadows under his eyes, and his cheeks were thin. The lower part of his face was like a rock, firm and harsh; and his brows were heavy and swollen. Before, he had played with his fingers, and toyed with his art; now he played with his heart and his soul. His youth was gone; he was a man. He had known life and suffered.

　　　　　　　Olive M. Briggs

She stared at him, and her hands were convulsed, clasping one another under the cloak. An impulse came over her to throw herself from the gallery at his feet, as she had flung the violets; and she crouched closer against the wall, clinging to it.

"Velasco!—Velasco!"

A roar went up from the House.

The sound of the clapping was like rain falling; a mighty volume of sound, deafening, frightening.

Kaya crouched still lower. He had taken the violin from his cheek and was bowing; his eyes scanned the House with a nonchalant air.

"Bravo—Velasco!"

The people were standing now and stamping, and screaming his name. They hid him, and she could not see. Kaya leaned forward, her gold hair gleaming in the light, her eyes fixed.

"Velasco—Velasco!"

Suddenly he started.

He looked up at the gallery and his bow slipped from his hand. He stared motionless. The first violin stooped and picked up the bow.

"Monsieur—" he whispered, "Monsieur Velasco, are you ill?"

"No—no!" The Violinist passed his hand over his eyes. "No—I am not ill! It was a vision—an illusion! A trick of the senses! It is gone now!"

He bowed again mechanically, taking the bow, lifting the violin again to his cheek. "An illusion!" he muttered: "A trick of the senses! God, how it haunts me!" He nodded to the Kapellmeister.

They went on.

* * * * * *

"Let me out!" said Kaya, "I am faint—let me out! Let me—out!" She struggled to the door, through the crowd, pressing her way slowly, painfully. Her cheeks were white and she was panting.

"Ah—for God's sake! Let me out!"

"Come this way, Velasco, this way through the passage. The din in the House is terrific—you have driven them mad! Hark to your name, how they shout it and stamp! They will be rushing to the stage door presently, as soon as the ushers have turned out the lights and the hope of your reappearance is gone. No wonder, man—you played like a god! You were like one inspired! Shall you risk it; or will you come through to my room in the Opera House, where we can wait and smoke quietly until the clamour is past?"

"Anywhere, Ritter, only to get away from that horrible noise!" The Musician covered his ears with his hands and shuddered: "That is the worst of being an artist—there is no peace, no privacy! The people consider one a music-box to wind up at their pleasure! A pest on it all!"

The two men quickened their footsteps, hurrying down the long corridor, and presently a door shut behind them.

"There—thank heaven!" cried Ritter, "Around to the left

now, Velasco, and then at the top of the stairs is my den. Let me go first and open the door."

The room was a small one, half filled with the bulk of a grand piano. About the walls ran shelf after shelf of music; opera scores and presentation copies in manuscript. A bust of Wagner stood in the corner, and on the wall behind the pianoforte was a large painting in sepia, dim, with strong lights and shadows.

The window was open, and below it lay the street, still in the darkness; above, the heavens were clear and the stars were shining. Ritter pulled forward an arm-chair and motioned the Musician towards it:

"Sit down, Velasco. Will you have a pipe, or cigar? You look exhausted, man! This fasting before is too much for you; you are pale as death. Shall I send out the watchman for food, or shall we wait and go to the Keller together?"

Velasco nodded and sank back in the chair, covering his eyes with his hand:

"Is it usual for musicians to go mad?" he said.

"Heavens!" exclaimed the Kapellmeister, "What are you talking about? Usual? Of course not! Some do. What is the matter with you, Velasco? You are overwrought to-night."

"No," he said, "No. When you hear themes in your head, and rhythms throbbing in your pulses—is that a sign?"

"Behuete! We all have that. After an opera my head goes round like a buzz-saw, and the motives spring about inside like demons. If that is all, Velasco, you are not mad. Take a cigarette."

"Thank you, Ritter. Tell me—when you conduct, is it as if force and power were going from you, oozing away with the music; and you were in a trance and someone else were wielding the baton, interpreting, playing on the instruments, not yourself?"

The Kapellmeister shook his head grimly: "Sometimes, Velasco, but not often; we are not all like you. That is Genius speaking through you."

"Afterwards," continued the Violinist, "it is as if one had had an illness. To-night I am weary—Bozhe moi! My body is numb, I can scarcely lift my feet, or my hands; only my nerves are alive, and they are like electric wires scintillating, jumping. The liquid runs through my veins like fire! Is that a—?"

"Bewahre—bewahre! You throw yourself into your playing headlong, body and soul. It wrecks one mentally and physically to listen; how much more then to play! If you were like others, Velasco, you would drink yourself to drowsiness and drown those sensations; or else you would seek pleasure, distraction. When Genius has been with you, guiding your brain and your fingers, and you are left suddenly with an empty void, what else can you expect but reaction, nausea of life and of art? Bewahre, man! That is no madness! It is sanity—normal conditions returning. You are mad when the Genius is with you, you are mad when you play; but now—now you are sane; you are like other men, Velasco, and you don't recognize yourself!"

The Kapellmeister laughed, drawing whiffs from his cigar.

Velasco uncovered his eyes: "You don't understand," he said slowly: "I see things—I have illusions! It is something that comes and dances before me as I play, the same thing

Olive M. Briggs

always. I saw it to-night."

"What sort of thing?"

Velasco stared suddenly at the opposite wall. "What is that painting there, Ritter?"

"The one over the piano? I bought it in St. Petersburg years ago, when I was touring: a copy of the Rembrandt in the 'Hermitage.' Don't you know it?"

"What is it?"

"The Knight with the Golden Helmet' I call it; but it is really a 'Pallas Athene.'"

"The Knight—the Knight with the Golden Helmet! That is no knight—it is the head of a woman, a girl; look at the oval of the cheek, the lips, the eyes! That is no knight, nor is it a 'Pallas Athene'!—My God! I am going mad, I tell you! Wherever I look, I see it before me—an illusion, a trick of the senses! It is madness!"

Velasco sprang to his feet with a cry. "I can't bear it," he cried, "open the door! Damn you, Ritter, get out of the way!"

Velasco sprang forward, struggling for a moment with the Kapellmeister, and then Ritter fell back. The clutch on his shoulder was like iron. He fell back, and the door slammed.

"Potztausend!" he cried, "What is there in my painting to start him like that? These musicians have nerves like live wires! It is true what he said—he is mad!"

The Kapellmeister went over to the painting on the wall and looked at it. "A girl's head," he murmured, "he is right. It is more like a 'Pallas Athene' than a knight; but if it were not for the helmet glittering, and the spear—"

Suddenly a remembrance came to him, and he struck his breast with his hand, crying out: "It is no knight! It is Bruennhilde, young and fair, with her eyes downcast! The light has fallen full on her face. She is standing there, and the stage is dim; her voice is still in her throat, dying away!"

Memory caught him then and he came nearer, shading his eyes with his hand, staring. "She has hung on my wall for years and I never knew it! It is she—it is her living image—her eyes and her brow—her lips arched and quivering! It is herself!"

"Bruennhild'!" He lifted his arms: "Bruennhild'!"

CHAPTER XXII

The sun came shining in through the garret windows, dancing over the floor in cones of light, caressing the geraniums until they gleamed a rich scarlet against the green of the ivy; and the cobwebs glistened like silk under the eaves. About the mill the doves flew in circles, alighting on the sill, clinging to the ivy with their pink claws, cooing gently, and pecking at the worm-eaten casement.

"Dear doves," said Kaya, "You are hungry, and when you come to me for bread you find nothing but the stone. Chrr-rp!" She whistled softly and held her hands over the sill, dropping crumbs: "Chrr-rp! Come, pretty doves, and eat!"

The birds came nearer, eying her out of their bright eyes with little runs forward, then circling and cooing again.

"Chrr-rp!" she called,—"Chrr-rp! Come!" And she held out her hands as if coaxing: "Come, my doves! Chrr-rp!"

One with fawn-coloured wings came flying and lighted on her shoulder; another followed.

"Come—chrr-rp!"

The soft little bodies huddled against one another on the sill, pressing closer; some on her arm and some eating out of her hand. She stroked their bright plumage, holding a crumb between her teeth.

"Chrr-rp—chrr-rp!"

The dove on her shoulder stretched his wings, pressing against her cheek with his breast, tipping forward on his pink feet, until his beak reached the crumb and he took it from her lips.

"Chrr-rp—chrr-rp!"

Kaya laughed softly, rubbing her cheek against the down of the bird; whistling and coaxing with her hands. The doves flew about her, lighting, struggling for footing on her shoulder and curls; and she shook her head, laughing:

"Chrr-rp—away with you! Would you pluck my hair and line your nests with my curls! Pischt—away with you!" she flung out the crumbs again. "There—eat, my pretty ones—eat!"

Below, the great wheel turned and splashed in the water with a whirr, buzzing. Kaya gazed down at it, and as she gazed she forgot the doves, and a strange little shudder went over her, so that the one on her shoulder lifted his wings in affright.

The water was deep in the pool, and there were little ripples under the spokes where the sun-beams were dancing. She dropped on her knees before the window and began to sing, still gazing at the wheel, the doves all about her, pianissimo—on the lower note of the scale, singing up, and then in arpeggios; each note distinct and separate like the link in a chain, pure, soft, hardly above a breath.

Olive M. Briggs

As she sang, her voice rose gradually, deepening and increasing in power. The doves pecked the crumbs on the sill, huddling against her and eating from her hands. She began to trill from one note to another, and in trilling, her thoughts ran hither and thither even as her voice, and her eyes wandered from the wheel, resting dreamily on the promenade, and the people walking under the trees.

The rhythm of a mazurka was in her ears and she sang louder, trying to drown it. She was in a great hall vaulted, dome-like with marble columns; violins were playing and the sound rose and fell, invisible as from the clouds. There was the perfume of flowers, heavy and languorous, and snatches of laughter, and the gleaming of jewels. The floor was shining and polished like a mirror, reflecting the forms of the dancers as they whirled to and fro. The light was dazzling and the colour.

She was dancing. Her feet flew in time to the rhythm. . . . Now it was dark and she was lying back on a divan, faint, helpless. The voice of the Prince was in her ears and he was bending over her; his eyes were crossed. . . . Ah, the clock was striking! It was midnight and someone had opened the door! Someone was crossing the room and bending over papers on the desk! . . . There was the sound of a shot! She was holding the pistol in her hand . . . It was smoking and through the vapoury wreathes she saw on the floor a body lying . . . a man on his face with his arms outstretched!

She shuddered again and the doves rose uneasily, circling about her, and lighting with fluttering wings.

"I have tried to atone," she whispered to the birds, "Come back! God knows—I have tried to atone!"

Then she went on trilling high up in the scale, her eyes

gazing dreamily and her hands amongst the doves, stroking them, playing with them.

Suddenly the door opened.

"Is it you, Marta?"

"No, it is I."

The voice was that of a man, deep and harsh, and the steps were firm. They crossed the room and stopped behind the kneeling figure.

"Hush!" said Kaya, "Not too near, dear Master! You will frighten the doves! See, how they press against me with their breasts and their wings—and how they flutter! They were hungry this morning, but they have eaten now and are happy. Once they came to me and I had nothing for them. If they knew better, poor doves, it is you they would fly to, and your hands they would eat from; since it is you who have fed them, not I."

"You were practising," said the Kapellmeister, "That is well, Kaya. I heard you from the promenade and I saw you. Your curls were like a halo of gold in the sun, and the doves circled, cooing. One was on your shoulder. Ah, it has gone now—I have startled it! It was close to your cheek, and you were feeding it from your lips."

"Yes," said Kaya, "Yes. It is sweet to be able to feed them. You have fed us both, dear Master."

She turned her head slightly, smiling up at him.

"Turn your head further, Kaya; let me see your face."

"The dove has come back. How can I? There—move a little, my dove—chrr-rp! Go away! No, he clings! See—I cannot! The down on his breast is so soft and his feathers so warm. He presses so close."

"Tell me, little one, how is your voice today? The same—full and strong as it was that night? Are you Kaya to-day, or Bruennhild'?"

The girl smiled again.

"Look at me, child. I have come to talk to you. There is a rehearsal this morning for 'Siegfried.'"

"Ah—yes!"

"The performance is advertized for tomorrow."

"—Yes?"

"Are you listening, Kaya? Your voice has a dreamy sound. What are you thinking about?"

She started. "Nothing!"

"What are you thinking about? Tell me."

"Russia!"

The Kapellmeister gave a sharp exclamation: "That is why you would not turn your head! It was not the dove, I knew. Are you still—"

"Yes," said Kaya, "Yes, it never leaves me. The curse, the curse of the—Cross!"

She pressed her cheek against the dove, hiding her eyes.

"It must leave you!" said the Kapellmeister roughly, "There is work for you to do! Rouse yourself, Kaya! Drive away the doves now or I will do it myself. If you brood, you will ruin your voice—do you hear me?"

"Pischt!" said Kaya, "Now they are gone—! I will not think any more of Russia to-day."

The Kapellmeister went to the window and laid his hand where the dove had been, pressing the slender shoulder and forcing her to turn.

"I want you," he said, "Now—this morning! I have come for you!"

Kaya rose to her feet slowly: "To sit aloft in the flies and sing while Siegfried seeks me?" She smiled up at him; "You have come for your bird?"

"No."

Her eyes searched his. "No," she faltered, "did I sing badly? I—I thought—"

"Kaya, the Schultz is ill."

The colour rushed to the girl's face and then fled away again, leaving her pale. "Ill!" she stammered, "You look at me so strangely, dear Master!"

"The Directors have authorized me to wire to Dresden for another soprano."

"Yes—?"

Olive M. Briggs

"I refused."

Kaya raised her blue eyes.

"I told them I had a Bruennhilde here on the spot. Can you do it? I have taken the risk. Can you do it? If you sing as you did that night—!"

"I will," cried Kaya, "I will!" She pressed against him like the doves, clasping her hands together. "It is only the one scene, Master; I know it so well, every note! Many times I rehearsed it with Helmanoff, many times. Bring me the helmet and the spear—bring me Siegfried!" Her eyes were shining.

"Then come with me now," cried the Kapellmeister, "As you are! Is that your hat on the nail? Put it on. The placards are out—and the orchestra sits in the pit, waiting. I have promised them a Walkuere with a voice like a bell! Come, Kaya—come! You are not nervous, little one, or afraid?"

Kaya ran lightly to the peg and took down her hat. She was laughing, and her face was alight as if the sun-beams had touched it; her lips were parted and the dimples came and went in her cheeks:

"Now—my cloak!" she cried, "Quick! Help me—the right sleeve, dear master, can you find it? Yes—yes! And my gloves—here they are!"

"Kaya, your face is like a rose and your feet are dancing."

She blushed. "You don't know," she said, "I have dreamed all my life of being Bruennhilde. When I feel the helmet and the shield on my breast, and the touch of the spear—it is like wine!" She stopped suddenly and passed her hand over her face.

"What is it, Kaya?"

"I forgot," she said, "I forgot—! Take my cloak; take my hat! I cannot sing. I forgot!"

Ritter stared at her: "What do you mean, child; what are you talking about? Is it fright? Tschut! It will pass." He took the cloak again and laid it about her shoulders: "Come now, the orchestra will be growing impatient. It is ten o'clock past."

"I cannot," said Kaya, and her lip trembled: "Telegraph to Dresden, dear Master—quickly!"

"Potztausend—and why?"

She backed slowly away from him and the cloak fell to the ground.

"Kaya, you shake as if you had a chill!"

"Can Bruennhilde sit aloft in the flies?" she said, "She is there in front of the footlights and everyone sees her. Oh—I forgot!"

"Donnerwetter! Of course she is seen! Is it the sight of the audience that will frighten you?"

"No," she said, "not the audience."

Ritter made an impatient movement forward: "What then? Sacrement! You were full of joy not a moment ago; there was no fear in your eyes, and now—it is as if someone had struck you!" He followed her to the corner where she had retreated step by step; and when she could go no further, he laid his hands on her shoulders.

"Look at me," he said, "straight in the eyes, Kaya, straight in the eyes. You must."

"I—cannot!"

"I tell you you must."

He bent over her, and she felt his hands bearing heavily on her shoulders; his eyes were flashing, insistent, determined: "You must."

"I cannot."

"Come."

She shook her head.

"Kaya—! You have been like my child! I—I love you as my own daughter! Your career, your success is dear to me. I have ventured more than you know on this chance—that you might have it. The town is crowded with strangers. The House will be full. They will hear you and your fame may be made in a night! What is the matter with you, little one?"

"I cannot," said Kaya.

His grasp grew heavier. "If you throw away this chance— listen to me—it may be years before you have another. You are young, and managers are hard to approach; you found that yourself. It is the merest accident of fate that the Schultz should be ill just now, while no other soprano is on hand, and you know the part. You sang it for me, Kaya, that night, and your voice was Bruennhilde's own. Would you be a coward now? Come, and let me cover you with the shield and the helmet; when you feel the spear in your hand the fright will leave you. It is not like you to be afraid, Kaya. Your eyes are like a doe's! Don't be frightened, little one."

She looked at him and tried to speak, but no words came.

"If I yielded to you, Kaya, if I let you be conquered by the stage-terror once, it would be a rock in your path forever. Come with me! My will is strong, stronger than yours, and I swear you shall come! If I have to carry you in my arms to the stage, you shall come; and you will thank me for it afterwards when the terror has passed."

"No—no!" The girl pressed closer against the wall, "Don't, dear Master, take your hands from my shoulders. I cannot!"

"Come."

"No."

He stared down into the blue eyes: "I tell you you shall come. You are throwing away the chance of a lifetime; do you understand? If you have no care for your own future, I shall care for it for you. Kaya!"

"No."

"Come, I tell you!"

His eyes were hard and cold, and her form was slight; it reeled in his grasp. She gazed at him and her chin was set like his own.

"If you care for me, Kaya, if you are grateful—" he hesitated, "Ah, come with me, Kaya! It is not fear I see in your eyes; it is something else. What is it? Tell me!" He put his arm about her shoulders suddenly, and the harsh look left his face: "Confide in me, little one, I won't try to force you. You are slight and frail, but your will is like iron; it is useless. If I carried you it would be useless."

Kaya took a quick breath. "Dear Master," she said, "It is not the audience I fear, not the audience, but it is someone in the audience. If that someone should see me and—and recognize me!"

"You forget, Kaya; did I recognize you?"

"No, but the foot-lights were not in my face. When the House is crowded and the curtain is up, and the glare is full in my eyes, then—"

"You are disguised by the hair red-blonde, and the helmet covering. No one could tell! At a distance you are not Kaya, you are Bruennhilde. Bruennhilde is always the same. When your eyes are hidden, Kaya, and your curls—the House is large—no one could tell!" He was drawing her slowly toward the door.

"You did not," said Kaya, "but—if he were there he would know."

"Who?"

She looked at him mutely, and he took his hand from her shoulder.

"Whoever it is," exclaimed Ritter harshly, "from the House, I swear to you, your own mother would not know you, unless she had seen you before in the part. That is nonsense! From the orchestra perhaps, from the conductor's stand—but not from the House. Kaya, you hurt me, child; you hurt me sorely if you refuse!"

He stood before her with his arms folded. "My heart is set on your success," he said, "and if—"

Kaya, looking up suddenly, saw that there were tears in his eyes. "Master," she cried. And then her will broke suddenly like iron in a furnace, red-hot under the stroke of the hammer. "You are sure?" she cried, "From the House no one would know me? You are sure?"

"I am sure."

She hesitated, looking away from him.

"No one?" she repeated, "not even—"

Then she raised her eyes and came closer to the Kapellmeister, looking up in his face. "He loves me," she stammered, "And I—I love him! But the curse is between us—if he should find me again—! Ah, it is myself I am afraid of—myself!" Her breath came in sobs and her face quivered.

The Kapellmeister lifted the cloak from the floor and put it around her shoulders. There was a strange light in his eyes. He gazed at her for a moment; then he caught her by the hand and drew her toward the door.

"Come!" he said, "Trust me, Kaya. I understand—at last I understand. Come!"

She yielded without a word.

They were both trembling.

CHAPTER XXIII

The second Act was over. The curtain had descended slowly, hiding the singers; the lights had flashed up, revealing the House. It was crowded from the pit to the gallery. The double row of loggias was ablaze with colour; and from them came a light ripple of talk and of laughter, broken loose as the curtain fell, a sound like the running of water over smooth pebbles.

The Schultz was ill. So it was advertized all over the foyer on huge yellow placards; and a new Bruennhilde was to take her place. The name was unknown; a young singer doubtless, brought forward under the stress of the dilemma. The audience whispered together and the ripple grew louder. In the next Act, the final scene, she would appear. The moments were passing.

Suddenly the door at the back of one of the loggias opened, and an usher ran hurriedly in. He gave a hasty glance over the occupants, and then bent and whispered to a gentleman in the rear.

"Monsieur Velasco?"

The gentleman nodded.

"Sir—the Kapellmeister has been seized with a sudden attack of giddiness and is unable to continue with the performance. He begs earnestly that you will conduct the last Act in his place."

"I—?" said Velasco.

"There is no other musician in the House, sir, who could do it. The Kapellmeister is in great distress. The minutes are passing."

"Tell him I will come," said Velasco, "I will come." He rose and followed the usher from the loggia.

When the curtain went up for the third Act, a young, slender figure appeared in the orchestra pit, mounting the platform; only his head with the dark hair falling, the arm raised, and the baton, were visible. The House was in darkness; a hush had crept over it.

The Act was progressing.

Already the smoke was in wreaths about the couch of Bruennhilde, hiding it, enveloping the stage in a grey, misty veil. Flames flashed up here and there, licking in tongues of fire about the rocks and the trees. As they rose and fell and the smoke grew denser, the music became more vivid, intense, full of strange running melodies, until the violins were to the ear as the flames to the eye. The stage was a billow of smoke curling, and the sound of the orchestra was as fire, crackling, leaping.

The smoke grew denser like a thick, grey fog, rolling in wreaths. The music was a riot of tones sparkling, and the hearts of the audience beat fast to the rhythm.

Suddenly through the veil, dim, indistinct, showed the couch of Bruennhilde, shrouded in the billows and puffs of the smoke; the goddess herself stretched lifeless, asleep; and the form of Siegfried, breaking through the ring of the fire, leaping forward, the sword in his hand. He sprang to the couch, gazing down at the sleeping Walkuere, straight and still, covered with the shimmering steel of the buckler, the spear by her side and the helmet on her head, motionless, glittering in the flare of the flames. "Bruennhilde— Bruennhilde!"

Siegfried lifted his voice and sang to her—he had taken the shield from her now and was bending lower, clasping his hands as if in ecstasy.

The House was like a black pit, silent, without movement or rustle, hanging on the notes, watching the glittering, prostrate form and Siegfried stooping. . . . Presently she stirred. The smoke had grown lighter, more vapoury, translucent. Her form stirred slowly, dreamily, raising itself from the couch. The magic was broken; the goddess was aroused at last.

Bruennhilde opened her eyes—and half kneeling, half reclining, she stared about her, dazed, half conscious. Siegfried hung over her. The flames, the smoke were dying away. She seemed in a trance; and then, as she gazed at the sky and the sunlight, the rocks and the trees, her lips parted suddenly; she raised her arms, half in bewilderment half in ecstasy, stretching them upwards, and began to sing.

It was like a lark, disturbed by the reapers, rising from its nest in the meadows. The notes came softly, dreamily from her throat; and then as she rose slowly to her feet, clasping the spear, it was as if a floodgate had been opened and the sounds poured out, full, glorious, irresistible, ringing through the darkness and the silence of the House. Drawn to her height she stood, the helmet tipped back on her red-blonde hair, the white robes trailing about her, the spear uplifted. As she sang her throat swelled, her voice came like a torrent: above the wood-winds and strings, the brass and the basses, the single voice soared higher and higher, deeper and richer, full of passion and pure.

"Heil dir, Sonne!
Heil dir, Licht!
Heil dir, leuchtender Tag!"

The "Heil" was like a clarion note ringing through space; like the sound of an echo through mountain passes. The audience listened and gazed as under a spell; the orchestra played as it had never played before; the baton waved. Siegfried sang to her and she responded; their voices rising and mingling together, every note a glory.

On the stage, still dim with the smoke and the flames, the light grew stronger, illuminating the helmet of Bruennhilde, the tip of her spear, falling full on her face and her eyes. She drew nearer the foot-lights, still singing, her sight half blinded, gazing unconsciously into the pit of the House and the darkness. She was clasping her spear, and her voice rose high above the violins.

Her eyes sought the baton, the face of her Master; and then as she stood, she trembled suddenly. Her voice died away in her throat; her steps faltered.

The Conductor leaned over the desk, the baton moving mechanically as if the fingers were stiffened. The orchestra played on. A shudder ran over the House.

What had happened? Bruennhilde had stopped singing. Siegfried was trying in vain to cover her part, singing his own. The Walkuere stood motionless, transfixed, her eyes riveted on the Conductor. A slight murmur ran over the House: "Was she ill—struck with sudden paralysis? Or was it the stage-terror, pitiless, irresistible, benumbing her faculties?"

She stood there; and then she stretched out her hands, trembling; her voice came back.

"Velasco!" she cried.

"Kaya—Kaya!"

But the audience thought she had called out to Siegfried, and to encourage her they applauded, clapping and stamping with their feet and their hands. The sound revived her suddenly like the dash of cold water on the face of a sleep-walker.

"I must go on!" she said to herself, "Whatever happens I must go on!" Her eyes were still riveted.

The face of Velasco was white as death; great drops stood out on his brows, his fingers quivered over the baton. He moved it mechanically, gazing, and he swayed in his seat as if faint and oppressed. The other hand was stretched trembling toward her as if a vision had come in his path suddenly and he was blinded.

Her lips moved again, and his. For a moment it seemed as if he were about to leap to the stage over the foot-lights. Bruennhilde fell back.

"For God's sake!" whispered Siegfried, "What is it? Are you mad? Sing—sing! Let out your voice—take up your cue! Go on!"

Again she cried out; but this time her voice was in the tone, and the emotion of it, the longing, rent the air as with passion unveiled and bared. She shook the spear aloft in her hands, brandishing it, until the gleam from the flames lit it up like a spark, and fell on her helmet.

Siegfried besought her and she answered, they sang together; but as she answered, singing, her eyes were still fixed, and she sang as one out of herself and inspired.

"Siegfried!"
"Bruennhilde!"
"Siegfried! Siegfried! seliger Held!
Pu Wecker des Lebens, siegendes Licht!"

The tempo quickened and the rhythm; and the tones grew higher and richer, ringing, more passionate. Such acting— such singing! It was as if the Walkuere herself had come out of the trance back to life, and the audience saw Bruennhilde in the flesh. The House reverberated to the sound of her voice; it was a glory, a revelation.

She sang on and on, and Siegfried answered; but the eyes of the Singer, and her hands lifted, were toward the House, the orchestra pit, the desk, the baton—the head with its dark hair falling and the arm outstretched.

The curtain fell slowly.

"Bruennhilde! Bruennhilde!"

With the flaring up of the lights the House was in an uproar. "Who was she? What was she? Where did she come from? Ah—h! Bruennhilde!"

They clapped and stamped, and shouted themselves hoarse,

calling her name: "Bruennhilde!"

* * * * * *

"She is there!" cried the Kapellmeister, "Go to her, Velasco; go to her quickly! Gott! I thought the Opera would have come to a standstill! My heart was in my mouth!—Go!"

He pushed the Violinist towards the door and closed it behind him; then he fell back against the wall and listened. The noise in the House was like a mob let loose.

"Bruennhilde! Why doesn't she come? Bring her before the curtain! . . . Bruennhilde!"

"I must go," he said, "I must speak to them—tell them any-thing—she is ill—she is exhausted! Something—it doesn't matter! I must go and quiet the tumult!"

The Kapellmeister leaned for a moment against the back-ground of the scenery; he looked at the door and listened. The House was going mad: "Bruennhilde! Bruennhilde!"

Then, staggering a little, with his hands to his face, he went out on the stage.

CHAPTER XXIV

"Kaya!"

"Velasco! Ah, Velasco! Don't come—don't touch—me!"

He sprang forward.

She was still in the Bruennhilde dress with the helmet on her head and the white robes trailing. The spear lay at her feet. He trampled on it as he sprang, snatching her into his arms: "Kaya!"

His grip was like a band of steel and he wound his arms about her, pressing her to him: "Kaya, my beloved! Ah, my beloved—speak to me! Open your eyes! Look at me!" He tore the helmet from her head and flung it to the ground. The red-blonde hair fell back, and he kissed her cheek and her curls.

He was like a whirlwind wooing, and she like a lily blown by the gale. She lay in his arms. Her lips quivered as he kissed them, but she lay without motion or sign.

"Are you faint?" he cried, "Have you swooned? Kaya! It is as if the world had gone to pieces suddenly and this were chaos, and only you and I—only you and I."

He kissed her eyelids.

"Open them, Kaya, they are blue as the sky."

He kissed her throat.

"It swells like a bird's when it trills, and the sound of it is as a nightingale in the twilight."

He kissed her lips.

"Ah, they are warm; they quiver and tremble!"

His arms were so strong she was pinioned, and she panted as she breathed. He kissed her again and again as one who is starving and thirsty, and she stirred in his arms, lifting her face:

"Velasco—my husband—my—self! To lie in your arms—it is heaven, and to leave them is hell! Let me go—Velasco! I love you—I love you! Let me—go!"

"So long as the world lasts and there is strength in my body—never! Say you love me again."

"I love you."

"You will never leave me? You will stay with me always while we live? Say it, Kaya! Your cheeks are white like a sea-shell; they flush like a rose when I press them with my lips! Say it, Kaya! You are trembling—you are sobbing!"

"I must leave you, Velasco—I cannot stay. It is like leaving one's life and one's soul!"

He laughed: "Leave me then! Can you stir from my arms?

They are strong. I will hold you forever." He laid his dark, curly head against the gold of her curls, and she felt his breath against her throat.

She opened her eyes: "My hands, Velasco—they are stained with blood; have you forgotten? How can I stay with you when there is—blood on my—hands?"

He pressed her closer: "Give them to me; let me kiss the stains!"

"I am cursed, Velasco, I am cursed! I have taken the life of a man!"

He held his breath suddenly, moving his face until he could see into her eyes. "Ah," he said, "Is that why you left me, Kaya, because of the curse?"

"Yes—Velasco."

"You loved me then! It was a lie? Kaya, tell me!"

"I loved you, Velasco, I loved you!"

"And now—?"

She clung to him and his arms tightened.

Suddenly he laughed again. "Hark!" he cried, "You hear the shouting? They are shouting for you! They are stamping and clapping for you; they are calling your name!" He threw back his head, laughing madly:

"Come—Kaya! Let us go together and peep through the curtain. The first time I saw you, you were there in the House, and I behind on the stage alone, with your violets.

Now we are together. You will leave me, you say? Come, Kaya, and look at the House through the curtain. You are trembling, little one; and when I put you down on your feet you can scarcely stand. You are sorry to leave me? It is like tearing one's heart from one's body while one still lives! Will you tear it, beloved? Come—and look through the hole in the curtain."

He put his arm about her, drawing her forward, looking down at her curls. "You are weak, Kaya; your form sways like the stem of a flower. Lean against me. Let me lead you. It is because your heart is so loyal and true; to kill it will be killing yourself! Don't sob, Kaya! Look through the curtain! Hark at the stamping! Look—dear beloved—lean on my shoulder and look!"

"Ah, Velasco, it is like a great mob; the Kapellmeister is there before the curtain. He tries to speak, but they will not listen! They are calling: 'Bruennhilde—Bruennhilde!' Is that for me?"

"For you."

"Why should I look, Velasco—why should I listen? My heart is breaking. I cannot bear it—Velasco!"

"Lean on my shoulder; look again, Kaya, put your eyes to the hole. Do you see a loggia above to the left, full of people standing, and in front some one tall and in uniform?"

"No, Velasco—I see nothing!"

"It is the tears in your eyes, Kaya! Brush them away and look once again. Don't you see him—in uniform, tall with a beaked nose, a grey mustache and his eyes crossed?"

"His eyes crossed—Velasco! Are you mad? He is dead! I tell you, Velasco, he is—dead! The Grand-Duke Stepan!—I killed him!"

"He is not dead."

"The Grand-Duke Ste—"

"He is not dead. He lives and he stands there before you—clapping and shouting your name."

She gazed up at him with trembling lips: "There is no curse, Velasco—he lives? There is—no curse—no stain on my hands? Am I mad? No curse of the Cross—the Black Cross?"

"Kaya—my beloved!"

She fell back slowly against his breast and his arms closed around her.

Choose from Thousands of 1stWorldLibrary Classics By

A. M. Barnard
Ada Leverson
Adolphus William Ward
Aesop
Agatha Christie
Alexander Aaronsohn
Alexander Kielland
Alexandre Dumas
Alfred Gatty
Alfred Ollivant
Alice Duer Miller
Alice Turner Curtis
Alice Dunbar
Allen Chapman
Alleyne Ireland
Ambrose Bierce
Amelia E. Barr
Amory H. Bradford
Andrew Lang
Andrew McFarland Davis
Andy Adams
Angela Brazil
Anna Alice Chapin
Anna Sewell
Annie Besant
Annie Hamilton Donnell
Annie Payson Call
Annie Roe Carr
Annonaymous
Anton Chekhov
Archibald Lee Fletcher
Arnold Bennett
Arthur C. Benson
Arthur Conan Doyle
Arthur M. Winfield
Arthur Ransome
Arthur Schnitzler
Arthur Train
Atticus
B.H. Baden-Powell
B. M. Bower
B. C. Chatterjee
Baroness Emmuska Orczy
Baroness Orczy
Basil King
Bayard Taylor
Ben Macomber
Bertha Muzzy Bower
Bjornstjerne Bjornson

Booth Tarkington
Boyd Cable
Bram Stoker
C. Collodi
C. E. Orr
C. M. Ingleby
Carolyn Wells
Catherine Parr Traill
Charles A. Eastman
Charles Amory Beach
Charles Dickens
Charles Dudley Warner
Charles Farrar Browne
Charles Ives
Charles Kingsley
Charles Klein
Charles Hanson Towne
Charles Lathrop Pack
Charles Romyn Dake
Charles Whibley
Charles Willing Beale
Charlotte M. Braeme
Charlotte M. Yonge
Charlotte Perkins Stetson
Clair W. Hayes
Clarence Day Jr.
Clarence E. Mulford
Clemence Housman
Confucius
Coningsby Dawson
Cornelis DeWitt Wilcox
Cyril Burleigh
D. H. Lawrence
Daniel Defoe
David Garnett
Dinah Craik
Don Carlos Janes
Donald Keyhoe
Dorothy Kilner
Dougan Clark
Douglas Fairbanks
E. Nesbit
E. P. Roe
E. Phillips Oppenheim
E. S. Brooks
Earl Barnes
Edgar Rice Burroughs
Edith Van Dyne
Edith Wharton

Edward Everett Hale
Edward J. O'Biren
Edward S. Ellis
Edwin L. Arnold
Eleanor Atkins
Eleanor Hallowell Abbott
Eliot Gregory
Elizabeth Gaskell
Elizabeth McCracken
Elizabeth Von Arnim
Ellem Key
Emerson Hough
Emilie F. Carlen
Emily Bronte
Emily Dickinson
Enid Bagnold
Enilor Macartney Lane
Erasmus W. Jones
Ernie Howard Pie
Ethel May Dell
Ethel Turner
Ethel Watts Mumford
Eugene Sue
Eugenie Foa
Eugene Wood
Eustace Hale Ball
Evelyn Everett-green
Everard Cotes
F. H. Cheley
F. J. Cross
F. Marion Crawford
Fannie E. Newberry
Federick Austin Ogg
Ferdinand Ossendowski
Fergus Hume
Florence A. Kilpatrick
Fremont B. Deering
Francis Bacon
Francis Darwin
Frances Hodgson Burnett
Frances Parkinson Keyes
Frank Gee Patchin
Frank Harris
Frank Jewett Mather
Frank L. Packard
Frank V. Webster
Frederic Stewart Isham
Frederick Trevor Hill
Frederick Winslow Taylor

Friedrich Kerst
Friedrich Nietzsche
Fyodor Dostoyevsky
G.A. Henty
G.K. Chesterton
Gabrielle E. Jackson
Garrett P. Serviss
Gaston Leroux
George A. Warren
George Ade
Geroge Bernard Shaw
George Cary Eggleston
George Durston
George Ebers
George Eliot
George Gissing
George MacDonald
George Meredith
George Orwell
George Sylvester Viereck
George Tucker
George W. Cable
George Wharton James
Gertrude Atherton
Gordon Casserly
Grace E. King
Grace Gallatin
Grace Greenwood
Grant Allen
Guillermo A. Sherwell
Gulielma Zollinger
Gustav Flaubert
H. A. Cody
H. B. Irving
H.C. Bailey
H. G. Wells
H. H. Munro
H. Irving Hancock
H. R. Naylor
H. Rider Haggard
H. W. C. Davis
Haldeman Julius
Hall Caine
Hamilton Wright Mabie
Hans Christian Andersen
Harold Avery
Harold McGrath
Harriet Beecher Stowe
Harry Castlemon
Harry Coghill
Harry Houidini

Hayden Carruth
Helent Hunt Jackson
Helen Nicolay
Hendrik Conscience
Hendy David Thoreau
Henri Barbusse
Henrik Ibsen
Henry Adams
Henry Ford
Henry Frost
Henry James
Henry Jones Ford
Henry Seton Merriman
Henry W Longfellow
Herbert A. Giles
Herbert Carter
Herbert N. Casson
Herman Hesse
Hildegard G. Frey
Homer
Honore De Balzac
Horace B. Day
Horace Walpole
Horatio Alger Jr.
Howard Pyle
Howard R. Garis
Hugh Lofting
Hugh Walpole
Humphry Ward
Ian Maclaren
Inez Haynes Gillmore
Irving Bacheller
Isabel Cecilia Williams
Isabel Hornibrook
Israel Abrahams
Ivan Turgenev
J.G.Austin
J. Henri Fabre
J. M. Barrie
J. M. Walsh
J. Macdonald Oxley
J. R. Miller
J. S. Fletcher
J. S. Knowles
J. Storer Clouston
J. W. Duffield
Jack London
Jacob Abbott
James Allen
James Andrews
James Baldwin

James Branch Cabell
James DeMille
James Joyce
James Lane Allen
James Lane Allen
James Oliver Curwood
James Oppenheim
James Otis
James R. Driscoll
Jane Abbott
Jane Austen
Jane L. Stewart
Janet Aldridge
Jens Peter Jacobsen
Jerome K. Jerome
Jessie Graham Flower
John Buchan
John Burroughs
John Cournos
John F. Kennedy
John Gay
John Glasworthy
John Habberton
John Joy Bell
John Kendrick Bangs
John Milton
John Philip Sousa
John Taintor Foote
Jonas Lauritz Idemil Lie
Jonathan Swift
Joseph A. Altsheler
Joseph Carey
Joseph Conrad
Joseph E. Badger Jr
Joseph Hergesheimer
Joseph Jacobs
Jules Vernes
Julian Hawthrone
Julie A Lippmann
Justin Huntly McCarthy
Kakuzo Okakura
Karle Wilson Baker
Kate Chopin
Kenneth Grahame
Kenneth McGaffey
Kate Langley Bosher
Kate Langley Bosher
Katherine Cecil Thurston
Katherine Stokes
L. A. Abbot
L. T. Meade

L. Frank Baum
Latta Griswold
Laura Dent Crane
Laura Lee Hope
Laurence Housman
Lawrence Beasley
Leo Tolstoy
Leonid Andreyev
Lewis Carroll
Lewis Sperry Chafer
Lilian Bell
Lloyd Osbourne
Louis Hughes
Louis Joseph Vance
Louis Tracy
Louisa May Alcott
Lucy Fitch Perkins
Lucy Maud Montgomery
Luther Benson
Lydia Miller Middleton
Lyndon Orr
M. Corvus
M. H. Adams
Margaret E. Sangster
Margret Howth
Margaret Vandercook
Margaret W. Hungerford
Margret Penrose
Maria Edgeworth
Maria Thompson Daviess
Mariano Azuela
Marion Polk Angellotti
Mark Overton
Mark Twain
Mary Austin
Mary Catherine Crowley
Mary Cole
Mary Hastings Bradley
Mary Roberts Rinehart
Mary Rowlandson
M. Wollstonecraft Shelley
Maud Lindsay
Max Beerbohm
Myra Kelly
Nathaniel Hawthrone
Nicolo Machiavelli
O. F. Walton
Oscar Wilde

Owen Johnson
P.G. Wodehouse
Paul and Mabel Thorne
Paul G. Tomlinson
Paul Severing
Percy Brebner
Percy Keese Fitzhugh
Peter B. Kyne
Plato
Quincy Allen
R. Derby Holmes
R. L. Stevenson
R. S. Ball
Rabindranath Tagore
Rahul Alvares
Ralph Bonehill
Ralph Henry Barbour
Ralph Victor
Ralph Waldo Emmerson
Rene Descartes
Ray Cummings
Rex Beach
Rex E. Beach
Richard Harding Davis
Richard Jefferies
Richard Le Gallienne
Robert Barr
Robert Frost
Robert Gordon Anderson
Robert L. Drake
Robert Lansing
Robert Lynd
Robert Michael Ballantyne
Robert W. Chambers
Rosa Nouchette Carey
Rudyard Kipling
Saint Augustine
Samuel B. Allison
Samuel Hopkins Adams
Sarah Bernhardt
Sarah C. Hallowell
Selma Lagerlof
Sherwood Anderson
Sigmund Freud
Standish O'Grady
Stanley Weyman
Stella Benson
Stella M. Francis

Stephen Crane
Stewart Edward White
Stijn Streuvels
Swami Abhedananda
Swami Parmananda
T. S. Ackland
T. S. Arthur
The Princess Der Ling
Thomas A. Janvier
Thomas A Kempis
Thomas Anderton
Thomas Bailey Aldrich
Thomas Bulfinch
Thomas De Quincey
Thomas Dixon
Thomas H. Huxley
Thomas Hardy
Thomas More
Thornton W. Burgess
U. S. Grant
Upton Sinclair
Valentine Williams
Various Authors
Vaughan Kester
Victor Appleton
Victor G. Durham
Victoria Cross
Virginia Woolf
Wadsworth Camp
Walter Camp
Walter Scott
Washington Irving
Wilbur Lawton
Wilkie Collins
Willa Cather
Willard F. Baker
William Dean Howells
William le Queux
W. Makepeace Thackeray
William W. Walter
William Shakespeare
Winston Churchill
Yei Theodora Ozaki
Yogi Ramacharaka
Young E. Allison
Zane Grey